India under Colonial Rule: 1700–1885

SEMINAR STUDIES   IN HISTORY

India under Colonial Rule: 1700–1885

DOUGLAS M. PEERS

PEARSON
Longman

Harlow, England • London • New York • Boston • San Francisco • Toronto
Sydney • Tokyo • Singapore • Hong Kong • Seoul • Taipei • New Delhi
Cape Town • Madrid • Mexico City • Amsterdam • Munich • Paris • Milan

PEARSON EDUCATION LIMITED

Edinburgh Gate
Harlow CM20 2JE
United Kingdom
Tel: +44 (0)1279 623623
Fax: +44 (0)1279 431059
Website: www.pearsoned.co.uk

First edition published in Great Britain in 2006

ISBN-13: 978-0-582-31738-3
ISBN-10: 0-582-31738-X

British Library Cataloguing in Publication Data
A CIP catalogue record for this book can be obtained from the British Library

Library of Congress Cataloging in Publication Data
Peers, Douglas M.
   India under colonial rule : 1700–1885 / Douglas M. Peers.
     p.   cm. — (Seminar studies)
   Includes bibliographical references and index.
   ISBN-13: 978-0-582-31738-3 (alk. paper)
   ISBN-10: 0-582-31738-X (alk. paper)
     1. India—History—18th century.   2. India—History—19th century.   I. Title.
II. Series: Seminar studies in history.
DS463.P44 2006
954.03—dc22   2005057754

10 9 8 7 6 5 4 3 2 1
10 09 08 07 06

Set by 35 in 10/12.5pt Sabon
Printed and bound in Malaysia

The Publishers' policy is to use paper manufactured from sustainable forests.

CONTENTS

INTRODUCTION TO THE SERIES

Such is the pace of historical enquiry in the modern world that there is an ever-widening gap between the specialist article or monograph, incorporating the results of current research, and general surveys, which inevitably become out of date. *Seminar Studies in History* is designed to bridge this gap. The series was founded by Patrick Richardson in 1966 and his aim was to cover major themes in British, European and World history. Between 1980 and 1996 Roger Lockyer continued his work, before handing the editorship over to Clive Emsley and Gordon Martel. Clive Emsley is Professor of History at the Open University, while Gordon Martel is Professor of International History at the University of Northern British Columbia, Canada, and Senior Research Fellow at De Montfort University.

All the books are written by experts in their field who are not only familiar with the latest research but have often contributed to it. They are frequently revised, in order to take account of new information and interpretations. They provide a selection of documents to illustrate major themes and provoke discussion, and also a guide to further reading. The aim of *Seminar Studies in History* is to clarify complex issues without over-simplifying them, and to stimulate readers into deepening their knowledge and understanding of major themes and topics.

ACKNOWLEDGEMENTS

We are grateful to the following for their permission to reproduce copyright material:

Plate 1 reproduced with permission V&A Images/Victoria and Albert Museum; Plate 2 reproduced with permission, British Library X 644 (24); Plate 3 reproduced with permission, British Library Add.Or.1.; Plate 4 reproduced with permission, British Library X 628 (16), Plate 5 reproduced with permission, British Library, BL W2126 (9) plate 9; Plate 6 reproduced with permission, British Library Add. 41300; Plate 7 reproduced with the permission of Punch, Ltd. www.Punch.co.uk, Plate 9 reproduced with permission, British Library, X 108 plate 11 'Cholera Camp' and 'For the Women' by Rudyard Kipling by permission of AP Watt Ltd on behalf of The National Trust for Places of Historic Interest of Natural Beauty; Edmund Burke, *Speech to the House of Lords on the Opening of Impeachment* by permission of Oxford University Press.

In some instances we have been unable to trace the owners of copyright material, and we would appreciate any information that would enable us to do so.

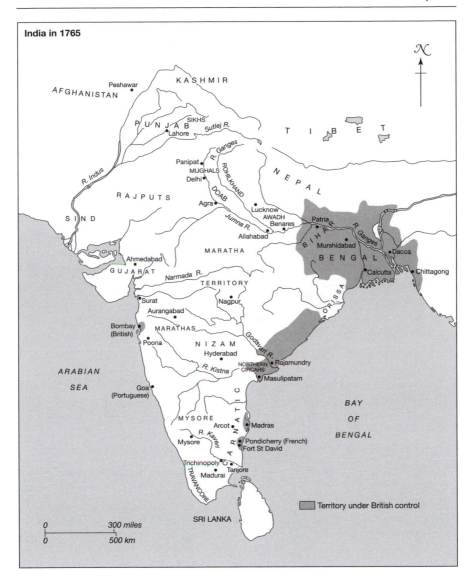

Map 1 India in 1765

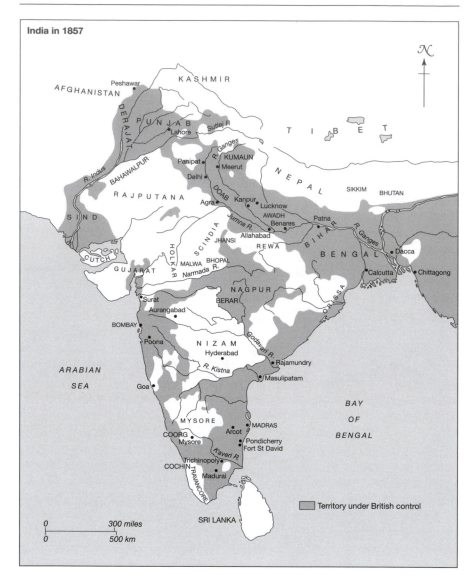

India in 1857

AFGHANISTAN
Peshawar
KASHMIR
DERAJAT
PUNJAB
Lahore
Sutlej R.
TIBET
R. Indus
BAHAWALPUR
Panipat
R. Ganges
KUMAUN
Meerut
Delhi
NEPAL
SIKKIM
BHUTAN
RAJPUTANA
DOAB
Agra
Kanpur
Lucknow
SIND
AWADH
Benares
Patna
R. Ganges
Jumna R.
Allahabad
BIHAR
CUTCH
HOLKAR
SCINDIA
JHANSI
REWA
BENGAL
Dacca
MALWA
BHOPAL
GUJARAT
Narmada R.
Calcutta
Chittagong
NAGPUR
ORISSA
Surat
BERAR
Aurangabad
BOMBAY
Poona
NIZAM
Hyderabad
Godavari R.
ARABIAN
SEA
R. Kistna
Rajamundry
Goa
Masulipatam
BAY
OF
BENGAL
MYSORE
MADRAS
COORG
Arcot
Mysore
Pondicherry
Fort St David
Kaveri R.
Trichinopoly
COCHIN
TRAVANCORE
Madurai

Territory under British control

0   300 miles
0   500 km

SRI LANKA

Map 2 India in 1857

One of the most common clichés is that India was the jewel in the British crown. This expression certainly captures how several generations of Britons came to see their empire in India. The British were proud, if somewhat astonished, at the rapidity with which they had secured control over most of the subcontinent, prompting one early historian to declare that 'The greatest fact, judged by the magnitude of its results, in the entire history of the world, is the establishment of the East India Company' (Kaye, 1852: 470). No wonder then that the viceroy of India, Lord Mayo, was moved to declare in 1913 that in Britain's possession of India lay the difference between being 'a first rate and a third rate power' and, therefore, 'Our national character, our commerce demand it and we have, one way or another, 250 million of English capital fixed in the country' (Misra, 1999: 21). Consequently, the history of modern India is a tangled history, one in which the histories of Britain and India are inextricably entwined. This is not to suggest that Indian history is merely a subset of the history of the British Empire. At the same time, writing the history of India without considering the dynamics of colonial rule runs the risk of ignoring the powerful effects – direct and indirect – that were occasioned by the experience of colonial rule.

The combination of pride and wonderment is a recurring feature of British writings on India and continues to influence writings on the history of modern India. The simple fact that a small number of British soldiers and officials, never totalling more than 1 per cent of India's total population, could first conquer and then control such a large and variegated society, was a source of pride and occasionally anxiety to the British in India as well as to British society at home [*Doc. 1*]. Moreover, the exotic qualities of India captured British imaginations and were expressed in British popular culture. Curry, for example, entered British cuisine in the eighteenth century, eventually becoming one of the most popular dishes in British society (Collingham, 2005). But, like so many other allegedly authentic Indian things, curry in Britain would have been unrecognizable to many Indians, an example of how colonialism could appropriate and transform even the most mundane objects.

What imperial rule meant to Indian society is an extremely complicated question as reactions to and understandings of British rule within Indian society were extremely diverse. In assessing how imperial rule affected India, there is widespread disagreement over just how extensive was that impact. There are those who insist that imperial rule had a dramatic effect on India (for good or bad), and usually Indians are presented in such works as either beneficiaries or victims of colonial rule, or if they are given any agency, they are shown to be largely reactive to forces beyond their control. At the other extreme are those historians who have argued that colonialism is but one of many forces acting on Indian society. Advocates of this point of view emphasize the dynamic interplay between colonizer and colonized, and stress the continuities between the pre-colonial and colonial periods rather than assume that colonial rule marked a traumatic rupture in Indian history. More recently, attention has shifted away from questions of cause and effect and in its place has come a growing interest in discovering what colonial rule meant to those falling under its authority. How, for example, did colonialism contribute to the fashioning of group and individual identities? One topic which currently interests many historians is the production of colonial knowledge, and in particular how constructions and representations of India emerged, and how these were in turn imposed upon India. Institutions like caste, which earlier scholars had treated as timelessly and inherently Indian, have been shown to have been largely the product of colonial efforts at classifying Indian society. Similarly, the origins of Indian nationalism have been revisited with an emphasis on how concepts such as 'nation' and 'community' were inscribed on Indian society.

The period under review here stretches from the beginning of the eighteenth century when the British began to break out of their coastal enclaves and ends in 1885 with the first manifestations of what would become the most visible nationalist movement in India, the Indian National Congress. As such it is a very conventional periodization, one which has its boundaries determined by major political developments. It is not my intention to suggest that high-level politics are the driving forces behind history, nor do I wish to imply that Indians were simply reacting to British initiatives. Nor do these dates denote watersheds in which everything changed – instead, as will be developed later, there were powerful continuities. But these dates do correspond, however roughly, to the shifting presence and priorities of the British in India and the ways in which Indians themselves adapted to changing political, social and economic situations.

NOTE ON SPELLING

There is a bewildering array of possible spellings for many Indian places and persons, not to mention Indian terms and concepts, and what standardization has occurred has been more by accident than by design. In many cases, the choice of spelling must be made arbitrarily. Wherever possible, antiquated spellings, except in direct quotations, have been avoided. But in order to lessen the distance between historical documents and this text, I have generally avoided the more recent (and linguistically correct) changes to some Indian place names and have instead chosen to identify them as they would have been known to earlier generations of writers. Hence, Bombay will be used in place of Mumbai, Madras rather than Chennai, and Calcutta not Kolkata. But other spellings have been updated; for example, Awadh rather than Oudh or Oude, Punjab instead of Panjab, and Marathas not Marattas or Mahrattas.

CHRONOLOGY

1707	Death of the Mughal Emperor Aurangzeb
1708	Rajput states break off from the Mughal Empire
1709	Afghan ruler Nadir Shah captures Herat and Kabul and presses on the Punjab (conquered in 1752)
1713	Nizam Asaf Jah establishes himself in Hyderabad
1733	Bengal is detached from the Mughal Empire
1742–51	Maratha Raids on Bengal
1746–61	Anglo-French rivalry in the Carnatic
1756	Siraj-ad-daula captures Calcutta from the British
1757	Battle of Plassey
1761	Marathas and Afghans meet at the Battle of Panipat
1763	Haidar Ali takes control of Mysore
1764	Battle of Buxar
1765	Treaty of Allahabad, Clive secures the *diwani* of Bengal and Bihar from the Mughal Emperor
1766	Hyderabad turns over its eastern coasts to the British, known as the Northern Circars
1769–70	Bengal Famine
1772–85	Warren Hastings, governor of Bengal (governor-general 1774–85)
1773	Regulating Act
1784	Pitt's India Act
1788–95	Trial of Warren Hastings
1793	Cornwallis introduces Permanent Settlement in Bengal
1798	Ranjit Singh made Afghan governor of Lahore, begins to build up his own kingdom
1799	British conquer Mysore
1802–05	Second Maratha War, British capture Delhi
1813	Company Charter renewed; loss of monopoly on trade with India
1814–15	Nepal War
1817–18	Third Maratha War
1820	*Ryotwari* system established in Madras Presidency
1824–26	First Burma War

1829	Abolition of *sati*
1833	Company Charter renewed; loss of monopoly on trade with China
1835	English made official language
1837	Accession of Queen Victoria
1838–42	Afghan War
1844–48	Sikh Wars, annexation of the Punjab
1848–56	Lord Dalhousie, governor-general of India
1853	Railways and telegraphs first introduced to India
1854–55	Santal Rebellion
1856	Hindu Widow Remarriage Act
1856	Annexation of Awadh
1857	Universities of Calcutta, Bombay and Madras founded
1857–58	Indian Rebellion
1858	India Act; end of Company rule
1861	India Councils Act; Council established to advise the viceroy which includes Indian members
1868	Punjab and Awadh Tenancy Acts
1871	First all-India census
1875	Arya Samaj founded; Muhammadan Anglo-Oriental College at Aligarh founded
1877	Victoria declared Empress of India; *darbar* held in Delhi to celebrate
1876–1878	Famine in Central India
1878	Second Afghan War
1879	Publication of Dadabhai Naoroji's *The Poverty of India*
1882	First Cow Protection League established in northern India; publication of Bankimcandra Chatterji's *Anandamath*
1883	Ilbert Bill
1884	Local Governments Act
1885	Inaugural meeting of the Indian National Congress

PART ONE INTRODUCTION

CHAPTER ONE

BACKGROUND AND HISTORIOGRAPHY

In studying the history of India under colonial rule, how it came about and what were its short-term and long-term consequences, we are confronted with a number of seemingly intractable paradoxes. First, how did a commercial company become a territorial empire? Constant injunctions to avoid wars of conquest were ignored. Officially, the East India Company, who represented Britain in India until it was dissolved in 1858, pronounced that it was opposed to conquests, for conquests were viewed as being inimical to trade. But it never attempted to roll back its frontiers. The British government also initially took the view that the Company was there to trade and not to fight. However, from 1750 onwards they proved quite willing to dispatch troops and ships to India to bolster the Company's activities. Secondly, how did the British become the paramount power given the limited resources at their disposal? What were the means by which the British were able to establish and maintain their authority in India, especially when the Mughal Empire was one of the most powerful, if not the most powerful, empires in the world at the beginning of the eighteenth century? And by means, we are referring not only to naked instruments of coercion like armies, courts and the police, but also the administrative systems, ideologies and economic policies, as well as the knowledge which was collected about India, for raw force alone cannot account for the speed with which the British achieved such commanding influence in India. A third question is how did a regime which increasingly identified itself at home and abroad with liberal principles end up pursuing such illiberal policies? In other words, why were British policies, or at least their consequences, so obviously at odds with the often noble objectives that they claimed to be pursuing? Such contradictions were not lost on contemporaries [*Doc. 2*]. These paradoxes will provide an overarching framework within which some of the fundamental questions of modern Indian history can be approached, particularly the hows and whys of colonial conquest, as well as the ways in which colonial conquest shaped the lives of those who were subject to it.

It is important to reject the one-time dominant image which posited a vigorous British Empire, equipped with better weapons and with more abundant resources at its disposal, against a moribund East wherein a deteriorating Mughal Empire was wracked by internal dissent, weakened by religious rivalries, and burdened with an oppressive and intolerant administration. A sense of inevitability pervades earlier attempts at understanding the colonial conquest of India, with its juxtaposition of the progressive West against the stagnant East. And yet, while we can easily discount the historical accuracy of such views, we must take care not to overlook their legacy, for the widespread acceptance of such interpretations not only informed historical judgements, but also helped rationalize colonial rule. Trusteeship, or a belief that more advanced nations have a moral responsibility to help 'backward' nations develop, depended upon these kinds of historical narrative. Even early Marxist historiography accepted the basic premise that the British, because of their more advanced economy, were inevitably bound to dominate India, and that such domination would break the chains of tradition that held India back.

Not everyone subscribed to such positive interpretations of colonial rule. By the end of the nineteenth century Indian historians were throwing up challenges, calling into question the allegedly noble motives of imperial rulers and bringing into sharp relief not only the contradictions within imperial rule but also its devastating effects upon local societies. Evidence was presented that over the course of the nineteenth century India was impoverished as a consequence of British economic policies and that the legitimate aspirations of the Indian people were being quashed [*Doc. 3*]. Yet nationalist writers accepted, at least in principle, the basic idea of progress, and rather than challenge the underlying philosophy of development, chose instead to highlight the degree to which practice had diverged from principle. For defenders and critics of empire alike, there was a tendency to exaggerate British power and influence and underestimate Indian resilience and innovation.

Views such as those identified above were ultimately grounded in the long-standing assumption that Indian society in the eighteenth century was in a state of crisis. This view needs to be reconsidered for not only did it ignore the many signs of cultural, political and economic vitality within India, but it served as a major rationalization for colonial rule then and now [*Doc. 4*]. Furthermore, from a contemporary Indian perspective, this description of endemic factionalism could just as easily be applied to the British who were also plagued by corruption, constant infighting, and even the occasional attempted coup. The image that Indian society was locked in chaos and crisis began to change in the 1960s and 1970s when a new generation of historians, less inclined to defend or castigate imperial rule, began to look more closely at the deeper social, political and economic developments under way in eighteenth- and nineteenth-century India. A much different view of Indian society began to take shape, one which emphasized its resilience, its capacity to innovate, and the transformations that were already under way prior to the arrival of British rule. Evidence was collected to show that the British were not acting alone, and that in fact the history of British India is a history of complex interactions. From this perspective, the British came increasingly to be seen as just another group vying for power and influence during a period of considerable flux (Bayly, 1988). An observer in 1700 would probably not have been able to predict the rapid contraction of the Mughal Empire and the emergence of a variety of new states in its place. Nor could they have foreseen the rapid build-up of British political, economic and military power.

In recasting the history of British India, historians broadened the scope of their analysis so as to consider the presence of a much wider spectrum of Indian society. Peasants and labourers began to figure in historical studies, and so too eventually would women and other groups that had hitherto been silenced. In doing so, however, historians encountered a number of methodological problems, not the least of which was how to recover the voice of millions of Indians who lived and died under colonial rule. It is a truism to argue that history is written by the victors, but in the case of British India, not only do most of the surviving documents emanate from British sources, and hence reflect their interests and assumptions, as well as the restricted scope of their vision, but there was also a widespread belief that in fact it was the British who brought an appreciation of history to India. Early British commentators on India were struck by what they saw as a lack of historical curiosity in India which only served to confirm India's stagnation [*Doc. 5*]. Consequently, the task of writing India's history took place within an intellectual context that was itself the product of imperial rule. Even early Indian nationalist historians framed their analyses within the terms of dominant western historical traditions, which is not surprising given that most of them were western educated.

Explaining why the East India Company embarked on a series of conquests is as difficult as explaining how. While certain individuals displayed aggressive temperaments, there was no clear broad-based commitment to conquest. Conquest was generally thought to be incompatible with commerce, and the Company, after all, was responsible to its shareholders. Many of the territories it acquired proved to be of little immediate economic value. There were exceptions of course – the densely populated agricultural lands of the Ganges Valley and the deltas of the Carnatic Coast were rich in revenues and the source of important exports. Nor did the British enjoy anything like a clear military superiority that would have encouraged risk-taking (Peers, 2003). An earlier generation of historians sought explanations in terms of Anglo-French global rivalry, thereby reducing the British conquest of India to the vagaries of European political rivalry. The upshot of the last several decades of historical work has been an appreciation that imperial expansion was the result of a complex interplay between British and Indian actors and institutions, involving a heavy dose of opportunism on all sides as Indians and

Europeans sought to maximize their political and economic potential through complex and ultimately unstable alliances. While conquest often failed to meet Company demands, and in some cases threatened its interests, Company officials (civil and military) could turn military action to their own advantage. Company officials became entangled in local economic and political networks by virtue of the private trade in which they were engaged.

If the history of conquest is best explained by focusing on the dynamic interactions between Europeans and Indians, so too is the history of the subsequent consolidation of colonial rule. The British Raj, at least for the first century of its existence, is best understood as a hybrid state for the British lacked both the means and the local knowledge to operate independently of Indian assistance. For all its pomp and circumstance, British rule in India was, at least initially, dependent upon Indian labour, Indian capital, and the tacit cooperation of key segments within Indian society.

Historians continue to debate whether colonial rule was an abrupt and immediate rupture or if it was instead just one of a number of changes which Indian society was experiencing. The tension between exponents of change versus those who emphasize continuities is captured in a recent collection of essays (Marshall, 2003) and can also be glimpsed in reactions to the publication of the *Cambridge Economic History of India* (1983) which critics accused of ignoring the impact of colonial rule on the Indian economy. Ultimately, the answer to the question of change versus continuity is determined by what is being measured, and the extent to which hindsight is allowed to enter our calculations. It is certainly true that the colonial state fashioned by the British in India had many of the attributes of the modern state. It developed a specialized apparatus for the collection of revenues, the acquisition and interrogation of information and the administration of justice. It was centralizing, paternalistic at times, nakedly brutal at other times. Yet, despite its objectives and authority, much of India lay beyond its grasp. The commercial and cultural transformation envisaged by imperial advocates was only incompletely realized, and that which did occur often ran counter to their expectations.

Two explanations for the paradox that the impact of colonial rule failed to live up to the reforming claims of British rhetoric (for good or bad) have often been advanced. (A third explanation – that India itself was so rooted in tradition that it could not be moved has fortunately been largely abandoned by historians.) The first has it that British rule, despite its rhetoric, was ultimately parasitic and rather than improve India, colonial rule crippled it. India became deindustrialized as government policy forcibly opened India to British textiles and killed off domestic production. In the countryside, revenue demands were cranked so high that many peasants were either forced off the land or so deeply impoverished that they were unable to free themselves from crushing debt burdens. Recurring famines and epidemics of cholera and the plague only made their lot worse. These experiences only served to accentuate the growing gap between what imperial rule promised and what it delivered, and not surprisingly there was a growing demand by Indians to have their voices heard.

Looking at the limits to rather than the potential of colonial power has provided an alternative explanation for this disjunction between what imperialism aimed at and what it achieved. The focus here is on the limited means available to the British as well as British anxieties: namely, a preoccupation with security and the fear of treading too heavily on Indian society. Ambitions were constrained by British apprehensions about moving too quickly and instead of embarking on sweeping reforms, as suggested by their rhetoric, they proceeded in a piecemeal fashion. Governed by a widely shared belief that Indian society was both ill-prepared for rapid change and ill-equipped to participate politically, the British chose to defend the practice of absolute rule and where possible try and operate within existing Indian practices and institutions, at least as they understood them. In common with many other liberal intellectuals of the nineteenth century, Sir James Fitzjames Stephen made an exception of India. Memories of the rebellion of 1857–58, plus a long history of viewing Indian rule as dependent upon a show of force, led him to argue in an article in *Nineteenth Century* in October 1883 that British rule was 'essentially an absolute government, founded not on consent but on conquest' (Stephen, 1883).

This is where the contributions made by post-colonial critics have become so valuable, for they have provided conclusive proof that much of what the British understood to be genuinely Indian was in fact the product of their own misunderstandings about the nature of Indian society, in particular the timeless essences which defined it such as religion, caste and tradition as well as the notion that Indians were historically conditioned to prefer arbitrary rule (Inden, 1986; Cohn, 1996). Hence, while colonial intervention was often presented in the guise of modernization and reform, British rule often had the opposite effect, that in fact British rule froze social and political institutions and frustrated indigenous evolution (Washbrook, 1999). Put another way, it can be argued that the impact of colonial rule was most revolutionary and transformative when it tried to preserve what it deemed to be 'tradition', for it often invented 'traditions' or converted practices into tradition when in fact they were far from widespread or widely accepted (Dirks, 2001).

PART TWO   ANALYSIS

CHAPTER TWO

EMPIRES AND ENTREPRENEURS, 1700–65

ENVIRONMENT AND THE PHYSICAL SETTING

Recent scholarship has shown a much greater interest in the ways in which environment and location have shaped the course of Indian history. The impact that distance had upon communications, for example, is an important determinant in modern Indian history for the time lag that affected the flow of news and information between India and Britain meant that British officials in India could not be so easily controlled from London, especially during the years covered by this book. The travel time between Britain and India averaged six months in the eighteenth century, which meant that as much as a year could elapse between a request for orders being sent to London and their response arriving in India. The introduction of steam propulsion and the opening of the Red Sea route dropped this time to three weeks by the mid-nineteenth century. The telegraph would later reduce the delay to a matter of days.

The influence of physical location and characteristics as well as that of climate are also widely recognized as having played critical roles in influencing Indian history. India's location in the middle of the Indian Ocean has meant that it has long been at the centre of a number of interconnected trading networks which encouraged traffic in goods and people, but also facilitated the exchange of religions and ideologies (Chaudhuri, 1991). Traders on the south-east coast of India developed extensive links with South East Asia, some of them travelling further afield where they left permanent reminders of their presence in such places as Angkor Wat in Cambodia and Bali in present-day Indonesia. Even earlier, the archaeological record confirms that goods were being traded between western India and Ancient Egypt and Mesopotamia. At the same time, the characteristics of India's seaward and landward frontiers have meant that it has been buffered against invasion from most directions save for the north-west and from the sea.

Within India, topographical barriers nurtured a number of distinctive subcultures. Forested uplands and deserts in western India separated much of the Deccan or central plateau from the northern plains, while the *ghat*s partly insulated the drier interior from the moister coastal lands. Mountain ranges to the north and west and heavily forested hills to the east have hampered the flow of goods and ideas in those directions. This is not to say that India has been isolated, for over the centuries it has had to contend with a number of invaders as well as more benign visitors. They came to India in one of two ways: overland through the passes that cut through the mountains that lie to the north-west between India and Afghanistan (particularly the Khyber and Bolan passes), or by sea. Those who came by land came to trade, to settle and to conquer whereas, until the arrival of the Europeans, seaborne contacts were nearly always peaceful. Historically, India has had only intermittent contact with Tibet and China to the north and Myanmar (Burma) to the east. To the north-west, there has been a longer and more sustained history of interaction on account of the passes that thrust their way through the Hindu Kush and other ranges stretching down from the Himalayas. These passes, however, do not allow for completely unimpeded traffic and they can instead be likened to turnstiles, permitting relatively easy egress into India for invaders coming in from Central Asia but then frustrating their subsequent efforts at keeping the lines of communication open with their homelands. Consequently, overland invaders have over time tended to become much more assimilated into Indian society as compared to the British, for example, whose control over the seas enabled them to maintain close links with their place of birth.

The monsoon has played a critical role in Indian history. Not only did the timing and direction of the monsoon winds in the age before steamships determine sailing schedules, but the rainfall that monsoons brought to India dictated agricultural practices. The foothills of the Himalayas as well as the fertile coastlands receive as much as 80 inches a year of precipitation; farmers in Bengal can expect nearly the same. By way of contrast, the Punjab and much of Central India get fewer than 20 inches a year. And further to the west, Sindh and Rajasthan receive even less. The volume of rainfall that came with the monsoon, and its timing, were two important determinants of the kinds of crops that were grown, as well as their yield. A third factor is the pre-dictability of the monsoon rains: some regions of India like Bengal not only could expect more rain but also could rely on the regular appearance of the monsoon (but should it fail, as it occasionally did, disaster was the usual outcome). Elsewhere in India, the Deccan for example, where monsoons were not so reliable, farmers turned to irrigation or the construction of tanks to forestall the threat of drought. Rice tended to be the major crop in areas with the greatest rainfall like Bengal; wheat and millet were favoured in drier regions in central and north-west India. Monsoons also affected warfare. As one British official observed, 'In India there are, with certain local variations, three distinct seasons in the year: the hot season, and the wet season, and the cold season. In the first, if you go to war, you stand a chance of being burnt to death; and in the second of being drowned. The third alone is fit for military operations; and it does not last more than four or five months' (Kaye, 1852: 462).

Within India's frontiers, there are three major geographical zones. The first of these is a densely populated plain stretching across northern India, reaching from the Indus River in what is today Pakistan to the delta created by the convergence of the Ganges and Brahmaputra rivers in present-day Bangladesh. Known historically as Hindustan, it was in this region that most of the great empires of the past originated, and even today it contains about 40 per cent of the population. Communications across this region were helped by the rivers. The western and eastern coasts of India were also densely populated regions, but, given their location, they tended to be more outward-looking and over time experienced an influx of merchants and traders from the wider Indian Ocean world whose descendants are still visible today in the various Muslim, Jewish, Parsi (or Zoroastrian) and Christian enclaves that date back in some cases more than a thousand years. The Deccan is a much more arid region and agriculture on the plateau is more dependent upon irrigation. Where rainfall was reliable, and crop yields easily exceeded the subsistence needs of the cultivators, such as along the Indus and Ganges rivers, there was more labour and social stratification as the land could easily support royal courts and their numerous religious and military retainers. Elsewhere, as in the Deccan, the carrying capacity of the land was more limited which reduced the possibilities for a densely populated, highly specialized and stratified society. In such areas, the difference between rich and poor was not as great as in the north, and more egalitarian forms of political organization took root.

Historians now appreciate that the environment has its own history, and that the natural world has not only shaped human societies but has in turn been reworked by human activity (Gadgil and Guha, 1993; Guha, 1999). Changes imposed on the natural world, with often catastrophic consequences, became particularly marked during the era of European imperialism when economic interests, technological means and a belief that the earth is ours to exploit converged. But compared to other regions of the colonial world, namely the Americas and Australasia, there was no demographic disaster to match that experienced by the original inhabitants of the New World. Imported flora and fauna did not displace indigenous species in India. Instead, new plants like the potato and the chilli pepper were added to the existing range of crops available. Nor did the introduction of European diseases occasion the tremendous loss of life observed in the Americas (the only disease of note that the Europeans appear to have brought to India was syphilis which they acquired from the New World). In fact, the pathogenic situation in India was tilted in favour of the indigenous inhabitants for it was the Europeans who found themselves threatened by the Indian environment.

Diseases like malaria and cholera took a dreadful toll on Europeans and, until medical advances later in the nineteenth century brought them more or less under control, death hung over the expatriate community (Harrison, 1999). Not surprisingly, disease was a common motif in contemporary British writings [*Doc. 6*]. Yet it would be erroneous to conclude that the European footprint in India was benign for, as we shall see, colonial policies forced major transformations in the use of land and in the ways in which human societies interacted with natural resources.

There is mounting evidence that India's physical environment experienced a number of substantial changes in the last five centuries. For example, the course of the Ganges shifted eastwards during the eighteenth century, with its westernmost tributaries like the Hugli becoming increasingly clogged with silt (Marshall, 1988: 3–5). Prosperous trading centres along its banks like Murshidabad suffered. The effects of deforestation partly account for these developments. So too do earthquakes in 1762 and floods in 1769/70 and 1786/88; the main branch of the Ganges was pushed eastwards, while the Brahmaputra moved westwards. As the two rivers converged, they formed an even larger delta which would prove to be especially hospitable to disease-bearing mosquitoes.

Imperial rule also made demands on the Indian environment. Indian forests became an important source of timber for the Royal Navy; Indian and Burmese teak were especially popular for teak was resistant to barnacles and therefore better and longer-lasting hulls could be built. Railway construction resulted in widespread deforestation: the demand for railway ties (or sleepers) and for right of ways and for fuel was staggering (Rangarajan, 1994). At its peak, railway construction in the Madras Presidency alone demanded some 35,000 trees a year. There were constant demands to bring forested and uncultivated land under the plough. These pressures were partly the result of population growth, and partly because the colonial government wished to bring waste land under cultivation so revenues could be extracted. It has been estimated that the population of India around 1750 was somewhere between 150 and 200 million. By 1871, the year of the first India-wide census, it had grown to 257 million (Kumar, 1983: 463–532). Much of that increase took place after 1820, for the previous seventy years had been ones of extensive famine and social dislocation which together slowed population growth. Pressures to bring more land under the plough, however, cannot be solely attributed to colonial rule. Certainly the pace quickened under the British, but there were already pressing demands with which pre-colonial regimes had to contend. Between 1700 and 1850, it is estimated that there was a 34 per cent increase in the amount of cropland in India, and that there was a further expansion of 38 per cent for the period 1850–1920 (Tomlinson, 1999: 67).

Colonial encroachments on India's forests fell especially hard on the various communities who had customarily occupied them. Many of these groups, known as *adivasis* (or original or indigenous inhabitants) in present-day India, found their traditional lifestyle of shifting agriculture, hunting and pastoralism threatened, and conflict often erupted between these communities and the agriculturalists and colonial authorities pressing down on them (Guha, 1990; Skaria, 1999). These forest-dwelling communities were known to British administrators as tribal societies, and while there is considerable debate over the appropriateness of the term (Guha, 1999: 1–8), so-called tribal peoples have certain distinguishing characteristics, including a symbiotic relationship with the land they occupy, a largely subsistence-based economy, and a relatively unstratified social and political organization built around loose family networks. They are also often distinguished by the absence, or near absence, of the kinds of cultural traits like caste that are associated with lowland peoples.

Colonial irrigation schemes are another example of environmental change initiated by British rule. Pre-colonial regimes invested in irrigation works, but the pace quickened under the British as canals promised to enhance agricultural yields. These schemes, once completed, would transform large parts of India, none more so than the Punjab where irrigation hastened social and economic changes. This commitment to irrigation was partly intended as protection against drought and famine as well as a means of increasing government revenues. But it served other purposes: in the case of the Punjab, it was intended to reward the province from which the British drew most of their soldiers and police (Gilmartin, 1994). The downside of these canals was that they not only proved to be excellent breeding grounds for malaria-bearing mosquitoes, but if not well designed they could increase the salinity of the soils and thereby in the long run make farming more difficult (Whitcombe, 1995).

MUGHAL ECLIPSE AND THE RISE OF REGIONAL POWERS

The long-standing argument that the conquest of India came about because of the transfer of Anglo-French rivalries from Europe to Asia no longer dominates discussion of the region's history. While few would deny the impact of European penetration on the course of events in India, reasons for the transformation and expansion of British activities in India are now being sought within India itself. Nor are historians as quick as they once were to assume that European domination of India was a foregone conclusion. That the British became the paramount power was by no means inevitable, for even by 1760 it is doubtful that any observer, British or Indian, could have foreseen that within forty years the British would become the dominant power on the subcontinent. Hindsight, however, now reveals that the eighteenth century was a transitional period; elements of the pre-colonial Mughal political and economic order coexisted, often uneasily, with the growing penetration of India by global influences. Simultaneously, this period witnessed the emergence of several powerful regional states, drawing upon distinctive cultural idioms and social patterns, and represented by a variety of linguistic and ethnic identities.

The dominant political power in India at the beginning of the eighteenth century remained the Mughal Empire, an empire that reached its greatest territorial extent about the time of the death of the Emperor Aurangzeb (1707). As far as empires go, the Mughal Empire easily dwarfed anything in Europe at that time, and European travellers were awestruck at Mughal wealth and power. It was infused with a military ethos that transcended ethnic and religious divisions and which, when coupled with Mughal administrative practices, enabled the Mughals to draw support from diverse communities within India, such as the Rajput princes to the south of Delhi as well as from the many soldiers of fortune who flocked to India in search of fame and wealth. Later commentators would make much of the fact that the Mughals were Muslim whereas most of their subjects were Hindu; while religious conflicts did occasionally surface, particularly under Aurangzeb who was much more religiously orthodox than his predecessors, the fact that the Mughals needed allies and that there was a common military culture kept such tensions largely in check.

At the centre of this empire stood the Mughal emperors, descendants of Babur, the ruler of Kabul who descended on northern India in 1526 (Mukhia, 2004). So impressed were European observers with the wealth and power of the Mughal Emperor that they attributed to him arbitrary and absolute authority, out of which would later come the theory that the natural state of governance in Asian societies was oriental despotism. In theory Mughal emperors enjoyed extensive power. But in practice there were a number of significant limitations to their authority. The size of their empire meant that discretionary powers had to be entrusted to their subordinates. They could not rely solely upon brute force and instead needed the cooperation of key sectors within Indian society such as bankers, local magnates and wealthy merchants. Even more important was that the Mughal state was so preoccupied with conquest that it lacked the will or the resources to penetrate deeply into Indian society. As befits a state in which war and ceremony were its most important pursuits, the Mughals maintained huge armies, in some cases numbering as many as half a million, and therein lay their focus of attention (Gommans, 2002). Provided that taxes were paid and there were no overt challenges to imperial authority, the Mughals were generally content to leave local matters in local hands.

To maintain its military momentum, the Mughal state needed a steady supply of revenues as well as recruits, and to achieve these objectives it employed a very sophisticated and, at least initially, successful administrative structure. The foundation of the Mughal state lay in what was known as *mansabdari*, a system of rankings or *mansab*s that differed from European feudal practices in that neither the rank nor the perquisites that accompanied it were intended to be hereditary, nor were office-holders entitled to permanent possession of lands (Richards, 1993: 63–6). Office-holders were assigned a rank or *zat* that specified the number of troops that they were to provide for imperial service (with the largest numbering in the thousands); in return they were given the rights to the revenues from a designated piece of land (*jagir*). Ranks were allocated by the emperor: he retained control over this system of rewards. Nobles were not given land grants, which could conceivably have given them greater autonomy; what they got instead was an income to pay for their troops and followers and support their lifestyles, which, because there was no incentive to pass it on to the next generation, encouraged conspicuous consumption that fostered the production of luxury goods throughout Mughal India.

In principle, *mansabdari* offered the Mughal emperors all the benefits of a feudal form of political organization but without its risks. They could raise large military forces, reward their followers and incorporate those willing to acknowledge their authority (and in so doing a multicultural aristocracy came into being), all without the dangers of creating a potentially troublesome hereditary aristocracy. In practice, the checks and balances that had been such important features of the system began to break down towards the end of the seventeenth century. Mughal expansion into the Deccan and further south had created a large and unwieldy empire over which the Mughal Emperor struggled to exert his authority. Efforts at maintaining central control were further undermined by the fiscal stresses experienced by the empire. In its earliest stages, the Mughal Empire had expanded into wealthy regions which easily met the costs of their conquest. This was not the case in the Deccan and, as Mughal military expenditures began to outpace revenues, office-holders saw their incomes decline. The Mughal state also stepped up its revenue demands which in turn stirred up resentment in large parts of the empire that, when coupled with religious and political rivalries, manifested itself in the emergence of popular movements such as the Sikhs in the Punjab or the Marathas in Central India. Local magnates, who had grown wealthy under Mughal rule, took advantage of fractures within the Mughal state to claim greater autonomy, laying the foundations for powerful regional states (Alam, 1986).

The Mughal Empire was not so much disintegrating as it was becoming reconfigured into a number of successor states, some of which were quite fragile and unstable while others demonstrated considerable adaptability and resilience. As a recent study has eloquently put it, 'From a balanced angle of vision the eighteenth century does not appear any more as a dark valley in the shadow of towering empires. What emerges is a mixed scenario of shadow and light, with high points and low points' (Bose and Jalal, 1998: 48). There is little substance to the image of Mughal India put forward by earlier generations of historians which accused it of succumbing to decadence, religious intolerance and in some instances personal depravity. While such negative impressions proved useful to early British writers eager to compare their rule favourably with that of their predecessors, the reality was nowhere near that simple. Merchants, warriors and investors were all scrambling to increase their own power and influence during a time of political flux and economic boom.

While the personal authority of the Mughal Emperor declined rapidly following the death of Aurangzeb, the outward forms and inner practices of Mughal rule would persist in the successor states that emerged in the early eighteenth century, even among Hindu regimes like the Marathas. By 1724, Asaf Jah, who ranked near the top of the Mughal hierarchy, had established a largely autonomous state centred on Hyderabad in Central India. One of his nominal subordinates in turn claimed the area around Arcot on the Carnatic Coast. By 1740, Bengal had passed out of Mughal control, followed soon after by the neighbouring state of Awadh (Barnett, 1980; Alam, 1986). Many of these rulers, seeking to enhance their own positions within such a fluid political situation, turned to Europeans for military assistance, not foreseeing the long-term consequences of such alliances. In return for European help, Indian rulers had to make concessions; sometimes these would consist of trading rights and monopolies, at other times they were forced to assign the rights to revenues from parcels of land.

During the twilight of the Mughal Empire we also find a number of regional powers emerging that drew strength from common ethnic and religious affiliations. The Marathas would become one of the most successful Hindu regional kingdoms, and proved to be potent opponents to the British. Under the leadership of Sivaji (1627–80) this coalition of pastoralists, cultivators and minor chiefs came together into a loose political alliance, linked together by their opposition to the Mughals and a shared language, religion and cultural traditions (Gordon, 1993). Sivaji would later become a powerful nationalist icon: his struggles against Mughal invaders became a metaphor for the campaigns undertaken by Indian nationalists against British rule in the late nineteenth and twentieth centuries. He would come to symbolize the struggle for *swaraj* or home rule. While religion certainly played an important role in binding this community together, one can easily exaggerate sectarian tensions. Not only did the Maratha elites adopt many Mughal practices, including the widespread use of Persian as the language of official and polite discourse, but large numbers of Muslims served in their armies.

As the area occupied by the Marathas lacked the deeply stratified social structures found in more densely populated regions along the Ganges, there were few barriers to popular mobilization. Lightly armed cavalry, practising hit-and-run tactics, pressed upon the frontiers of the Mughal state in the seventeenth century, and laid the foundations for a confederacy that at its peak stretched across much of northern and central India. The Mughals failed to overawe the Marathas, and in the political turbulence of the early eighteenth century the hereditary chief ministers or *peshwa*s of Sivaji and his successors, drawn from the Chitpavan Brahmin community, sought to consolidate their authority over the wider Maratha community. The *peshwa*s, however, never gained complete control over the various warrior chiefs in the countryside, and the subsequent history of the Marathas was one in which their formidable military talents were often undermined by struggles between the various warrior chiefs, and between them and the *peshwa*s.

The Sikhs make their first appearance as a distinctive religious community in the Punjab at the beginning of the sixteenth century. Their religious beliefs and practices drew upon Sufism as well as Hindu *bhakti*, both of which appealed to those seeking a more personalized religious experience. Peasants, farmers and traders in this region were drawn to the religious teachings and personal examples set by a series of teachers or gurus. Initially, the emphasis was on creating an egalitarian community, one which rejected the social hierarchies associated with the Hindu caste system. It was also a community that favoured peaceful coexistence. However, the combination of religious persecution (a number of the gurus were murdered by Mughal authorities) as well as the strategic region of India they occupied meant that they were frequently forced to defend their lands and their faith. By 1708, the year in which the last of the gurus, Guru Govind Singh, died, the *khalsa*, or army of the pure, had been formed (Grewal, 1991). The rise of the Sikhs as a major regional power accelerated under the leadership of Ranjit Singh who was able to use his position in Lahore and the forces under his command to weld together the Sikhs in the Punjab into a single state.

The early eighteenth century was a time when social identities were still largely tied to particular places. Particular landed castes dominated specific regions. Sometimes a single group dominated a region as was the case with the Marathas; in other areas, a more complicated mix of groups jostled for political and economic power as happened in Bengal, where Brahmins, Mughal nobles, Rajput warriors and rich merchants competed with each other. Within each region, the constituent communities were ranked hierarchically. This provided the basis for the caste system, but caste identities, and their respective rankings were neither as timeless nor as static as many British observers came to believe (Bayly, 1999). Societies were also very patriarchal, with gender relations being conditioned by a combination of social customs, property rights and religious rituals. The growing power of warrior groups in some regions, for example, placed a premium on the maintenance of particular forms of female virtue. The lives of women in such areas were much more circumscribed as *purdah* or the practice of secluding women from public life grew in importance. Matrimonial exchanges within these communities helped to buttress relations between nobles and their followers, as well as cement alliances between allied groups. Such marriages often crossed religious lines, indicating that religious boundaries were often secondary to dynastic priorities. Expansionary pressures unleashed during this era also pressed heavily on the more isolated and marginalized communities inhabiting the less accessible forest lands scattered about the subcontinent. Pastoral and nomadic groups found their freedoms curtailed as they came into conflict with sedentary societies.

The surest proof of the implosion of Mughal authority came with a series of invasions that rocked the Mughal heartland around Delhi. Persian invaders led by Nadir Shah sacked Delhi in 1739, seizing the fabled Peacock Throne which he hauled back to Iran. In 1757, an Afghan army managed to capture the Mughal Emperor, an event overshadowed in western historiography by the Battle of Plassey fought that same year between the British and the Nawab of Bengal. One of the bloodiest battles in the eighteenth century took place at Panipat, near Delhi, in 1761 when Maratha forces tried to rebuff an attempt made by the Afghans to retain their control over the Mughal Emperor. There was no clear victor in this battle. The Marathas made a number of tactical blunders and suffered terrible losses which ultimately frustrated Maratha attempts to become the dominant power in north India. But the Afghans were seriously bloodied and they too found that they could not consolidate their authority. Events such as these illustrate not only just how many groups were competing for authority, but also the extent to which subsequent developments in India were determined by events in which Europeans played no role.

EUROPEANS AND THE TRADING WORLD OF THE INDIAN OCEAN

India's wealth had long seduced traders and warriors who came to India by sea and by land to make their fortunes. They discovered a vast and complex trading world which linked states from around the Indian Ocean and beyond with each other. India had long been a regional hub, partly because of its location astride the major seaborne trade routes, partly because of the goods that India itself produced and exported throughout the region, and partly because in India could be found the skills and the capital necessary to embark on extensive trading ventures. In addition to luxury fabrics made of silk and finely finished cotton, there was a huge trade in coarser goods intended for mass consumption. When the Portuguese touched shore at Calicut in 1498 (an event which European historiography has blown all out of proportion), they found a flourishing economy already in place, one with which they were unable to compete on equal terms for they had little to offer (Chaudhuri, 1985). The goods that could be brought from Europe were all too often seen as crude or unsuited to Indian tastes. Their Dutch, British and French rivals would face similar challenges. But the lure of Indian and Asian commodities, spices and textiles in particular, was just too tempting. Precious metals were one way of securing these goods, and there is plenty of evidence to suggest that a good portion of the mineral wealth mined in the New World found its way to India. But Europeans were reluctant to distribute too much of their scarce bullion in foreign markets, and so had to find other strategies to crack open eastern markets.

What distinguished the Portuguese most from other traders active in the Indian Ocean was both their willingness and capacity to use force to achieve their ends. This is not to say that the trading world of the Indian Ocean was free from violence. It existed, but the violence that did occur was individualistic in nature and not state sponsored or sanctioned. Unlike the Mediterranean, which had grown progressively more militarized owing to intense European competition, the states bordering the Indian Ocean had historically shown little interest in becoming involved in promoting or protecting ocean-going trade. The ethos of the marketplace clashed with the chivalric and militarized culture of the ruling aristocracy. Political and commercial activities were kept much more distinct in India than was the case, for example, in Holland or Great Britain. European political and legal systems were much more geared towards supporting and encouraging capital than was the case in many of the major Asian states where merchants often prospered despite, rather than because of, the region's political regimes (Chaudhuri, 1985: 209–17).

The arrival of the Portuguese initiated a series of changes that would have profound ramifications for the whole region. But a word of caution is in order: the long-standing tradition of assuming that Europeans were the principal force for change in world history has led us to exaggerate their early impact on the Indian Ocean. Indian traders were more adversely affected by the decline of Safavid and Mughal empires than by the beginnings of European empires, and, as we have already touched upon, the fall of the Mughal Empire and the rise of the British Empire were only indirectly related. Hence, the importance of the Portuguese was not so much what they did, but rather what they pointed towards. In other words, they were harbingers of things to come. The Portuguese, eager for access to the fabled riches of the East, found that they had little with which they could peacefully and profitably trade. But they did have well-armed sailing vessels and, more importantly, they were willing to use them to carve out a position for themselves in the region (Scammell, 1996). Their zeal was further stoked by religious antagonisms against Muslims, a legacy of centuries of struggles in the Mediterranean.

The dominant position established by the Portuguese was, however, short-lived; by the seventeenth century the Dutch had overtaken them (Subrahmanyam, 1992). Dutch success can be accounted for by a number of factors, including superior commercial organization and a tendency not to let religious zeal interfere with turning a profit. However, the Dutch and British were quite willing to use force to back up the activities of their merchants. British traders came hard on the heels of the Dutch, but they were not as successful at the outset. Both the Dutch and the British governments relied upon private enterprise to gain access to eastern markets, but, in keeping with the principles of mercantilism, the Dutch and British each established chartered corporations which were given a monopoly over trade with the region (Furber, 1976; Lawson, 1993). Dutch, English and eventually French traders in the region followed the prevailing customs and traditions in the Indian Ocean whereby foreign merchants were allowed to set up trading factories in port cities where they were entitled to conduct trade and keep their own religious and cultural practices as long as they did not disturb others.

At the outset, the Dutch East India Company's capital investments were ten times that of the English East India Company (founded in 1600), and it also managed through diplomacy and force to prevent the British from becoming established in what was then the most lucrative market: present-day Indonesia from where most of the spices came. Squeezed out of what is today Indonesia by the more powerful Dutch, the English East India Company (EIC) was forced to fall back on India. What might have appeared at the time to have been a consolation prize would in the long run be to the advantage of the British as they learned to tap into the lucrative trade in textiles, both between Asia and Europe as well as within Asia. The initial objectives of the EIC were to secure access to the spice trade and find markets for English woollens which were then one of Britain's largest exports. Initially, demand for Indian textiles was quite limited. Luxury items like shawls and wall hangings were introduced in small numbers, but large quantities of Indian textiles did not begin to enter the British Isles until the second half of the seventeenth century. Cotton piecegoods from India were popular because they were cheap, relatively durable, and more easily washed than linen and wool cloth. In the words of one historian, 'At the turn of the eighteenth century, India was probably the largest and most cost-competitive textile-manufacturing country in the world' (Prakash, 1998: 349). Data that has been collected on the composition of the EIC's imports into Europe over the course of the eighteenth century confirms the dominant position enjoyed by textiles but also the growing importance of other commodities. At the beginning of the eighteenth century, textiles comprised 74 per cent of the total imports coming into Europe; by 1760 they had fallen to 54 per cent. The most spectacular growth was that of tea: jumping from a shade over 1 per cent in 1700 to 25 per cent in 1760 (Prakash, 1998: 122). While tea would not be grown in India until the nineteenth century when plantations were opened in Assam and in the Nilgiri hills of southern India, the Company purchased tea from China through its exports of opium, cotton and an assortment of other commodities to China. Tea proved to be a major source of profits for the EIC, and for the British government which levied taxes on its consumption.

In both the scope of its activities as well as the wealth it generated, the English East India Company can be seen as the prototype of today's multinational corporation. By 1700, imports from Asia were equal in value to those from the West Indies, and double those from North America (Price, 1998: 101). India remained a major exporter of finished cotton goods up until the 1820s, when the advent of machine production in the United Kingdom allowed manufacturers there to produce cotton goods at an even lower price, many of which would be destined for Indian markets. Trade with India not only provided items for sale in the home market, but the commodities exported from India and the returns on investments made in India enabled the British to strengthen wider imperial trading networks. Textiles from India played an important role in the slave trade which Britain also came to dominate, as Indian cloth was sent to Africa where it was used to purchase slaves. All this begs the question of whether there existed a direct and causal link between the growth in trade and the subsequent conquest of India. At one point, many argued that there was a direct relationship – a conspiracy of sorts that could either be attributed to the cunning plans of British statesmen or the inevitability of capitalist development (Mukherjee, 1982; Chaudhury, 1995). A closer examination of developments in India suggests that, while the two were not unrelated, it was not inevitable that the flag would follow hard on the heels of trade.

The desire for cotton goods and spices is not by itself sufficient to account for the transformation of the British from traders to territorial rulers. While industrializing Britain did come to benefit from its ability to control Indian markets, during the early and crucial flurry of conquests British manufacturing and commercial interests were either oblivious to India or championed peace. The EIC lamented the aggressive actions of its officials in India and sought to limit its military commitments to the area. Until the mid-eighteenth century, the Company's military forces in India consisted of small packets of ill-trained European troops and even more poorly trained Indian auxiliaries. There was usually no more than a hundred of each at the Company's major factories, and their primary function was to protect the factories from robbers and post guards on convoys heading inland. There was, however, one notable early exception and that came when an ill-fated attempt was made to use force to enhance the Company's presence in Bengal. A small force was sent by the EIC to capture Chittagong and Salsette. When this force arrived in the Hugli in October 1686, it was easily beaten back, and Aurangzeb ordered an attack on British factories in areas under his authority. Following payment of a fine of £15,000, the East India Company had its trading privileges restored (Lawson, 1993: 49–50). It was in all respects a setback, and the Company would in future try, not always successfully, to curb its officials' ambitions.

COMPETITION AND CONFLICT IN SOUTH INDIA

Through the course of the seventeenth century and early eighteenth century, Europeans eager to penetrate the lucrative markets of the Indian Ocean began to establish coastal enclaves. The English East India Company established a string of trading factories along the east and west coasts of India, including a number that would become springboards into the interior (Bengal, Madras and Bombay). And as we have already seen, these initial forays into India coincided with the major upheavals in India's political landscape. Asaf Jah, the Nizam of Hyderabad, made several decisions just prior to his death in 1748 which, when viewed with the benefit of hindsight, were clearly to have momentous consequences. Much of his attention was directed to the southern coasts which had been enriched by trade in textiles and rice. This, however, brought him into sharp conflict with his nominal subordinate, the Nawab of the Carnatic, who like Asaf Jah was busily trying to build up an independent power base. The situation was further complicated with the appearance of a Maratha army, intent on securing *chauth* and establishing its own claim to the area. In order to shore up his authority and defeat his rivals, Asaf Jah turned to French capital and French soldiers for assistance. This in turn encouraged his enemies to seek the assistance of the British, who were faced with the choice of doing nothing and risk having the French achieve commanding influence, or joining in.

The French were relative late arrivals to the trading world of Asia (the Compagnie des Indes Orientales was founded in 1664) but they vigorously sought to expand their trading activities in southern India in the first half of the eighteenth century. From their base at Pondicherry on the east coast, and later from Chandernagore in Bengal, French officials embarked on a risky strategy which combined political and military intervention with increased commercial activity as a means of bolstering trade and undermining their British rivals. Key to French designs were the plans made by their governor, Joseph-François Dupleix (1697–1763), who was willing to involve the French in local politics as a way of improving their position (Sen, 1947). The fact that the British and French governments were frequently at war with one another in Europe heightened tensions between the two companies. Dupleix took the lead by aligning himself with local magnates in their pursuit of local power. He raised a corps of Indian recruits, disciplining and organizing them along European lines. While infantry was not unknown in India, the predominant military culture throughout much of India stressed a more individualistic style of warfare, emphasizing cavalry in particular (Gordon, 1998). The British and French also popularized light field artillery that could accompany the infantry, rather than the large and spectacular siege guns that were commonplace in many Indian armies. However, in order to maintain European-style infantry in a peak state of discipline, they needed to be paid regularly, and hence the French and those who emulated them in raising similar military formations were required to develop better revenue pumps in order to ensure a steady flow of cash. Access to land revenues became even more crucial.

It was the kind of military organization that Europeans brought to India, as well as ensuring sufficient resources to sustain it, which marked the real difference between them and the armies of the Indian powers with whom they were either allied or in conflict (Lenman, 2000). The weapons available to the Europeans did not differ much from those used by their Indian allies and Indian opponents. Flintlock muskets, muzzle-loading iron and brass cannon and swords were found throughout India. Indian armies proved themselves to be very adaptable, and over time they began to assimilate aspects of western ways of warfare just as British military forces in India would take on a hybrid character (Cooper, 2003; Peers, 2003).

The speed with which the British responded to these French inroads can be partly accounted for by the British need to forestall any French threat to their trade in textiles. In the 1720s French profits were only about 50 per cent of those enjoyed by the British; by the late 1730s the French were coming close to parity (Marshall, 1998). Southern India at this time was an important market for the textile trade which had become so crucial to British trade. While the French might have taken the initiative, the British enjoyed a number of advantages which eventually allowed them by the late 1760s to contain French ambitions and roll back the gains that they had made. The British government had by mid-century concluded that what was in the Company's interest was in the national interest, and hence were more willing to provide the kind of consistent support to the Company that enabled it to function despite the serious challenges it faced. Of these, the presence of the Royal Navy was critical for it allowed the British to move resources around India more quickly by sea as well as to frustrate French efforts at bringing in reinforcements.

Increased European military activity in India can be explained by the convergence of two initially unrelated developments: the desire by Indian rulers for military assistance as they pursued their own political ambitions, and the intensity of Anglo-French political and commercial rivalry which encouraged their officials in India to take advantage of the opportunities which presented themselves to gain the upper hand over their rivals. There was so far no clearly articulated theory of empire at work; the EIC was primarily interested in the bottom line, which in their eyes was determined by trade and not through conquest. Yet these initial alliances between the EIC and Indian rulers set in motion a chain of events that would leave the British in a dominant position. The costs of providing military support to Indian rulers could become very expensive, and Indian rulers were expected to pay handsomely for European military support. Some of that would come from offers of increased trading privileges, but most would come from promises that land revenues would be turned over to them. Indian rulers were often unable, and sometimes unwilling, to honour their offers and promises, in which case the

Europeans would use their military and political clout to demand that actual lands be turned over to them to cover the costs that had been incurred.

The situation became even more volatile when the personal interests of Company officials were factored into the equation. A good number of the most lucrative trading opportunities had passed into the hands of Europeans acting on their own, despite the Company's efforts to curb them (Marshall, 1976). Their officials in India had access to political power and influence, and extensive trading networks, yet they often lacked ready capital and hence turned to Indian investors to provide it. This heightened tensions as Company officials acting on their own often demanded and acted upon the privileges that had been granted to their employer and not to them personally. Distance, as noted before, frustrated the Company's efforts to keep close tabs on its officials, as did the lack of a well-organized and professional bureaucracy in India. The authority of Indian rulers suffered as they were trapped by their growing dependency on European assistance and confronted by a loss of control over the commercial and financial transactions occurring in their kingdoms.

As British influence and, eventually, authority began to filter outwards from the coast and into the interior of southern India, it put the British on a collision course with the state of Mysore. This state would prove to be one of the biggest challenges to British rule in India on account not only of its strategic location, but also because of the skill with which its rulers were able to mobilize opposition to the British (Habib, 1999). Up until 1763, Mysore had been a relatively small state, ruled by a Hindu dynasty, which had not shown interest in expansion. However, in 1763 a coup was mounted by Haidar Ali, a Muslim general from the north who, like so many others, had sought his fortune in the service of the many smaller kingdoms dotted about central and southern India. Haidar Ali and his son, Tipu Sultan, who succeeded him in 1782, created an efficient and loyal bureaucracy and a well-equipped and trained army that was backed by a sophisticated revenue administration. With such resources at their disposal, Mysore mounted a number of devastating attacks on the territories of the British and their allies. In strengthening and modernizing his regime, Haidar Ali was careful not to alienate powerful Hindu merchant interests, and with their support he was able to bolster his authority and build an effective revenue system. And contrary to British efforts to depict him as a typical tyrant and religious bigot, Haidar Ali appears to have been largely uninterested in religious affairs and was able to draw support from Hindus and Muslims alike.

THE REVOLUTION IN BENGAL

If we were to identify any single development that can account for Britain's rise to paramountcy in India, it would have to be the conquest of Bengal, for not only did its possession provide Britain with the revenues and the labour with which it could transform itself from a trading enterprise into a territorial power, just as importantly it stimulated officials to begin to think imperially. What began in 1756 in a campaign to restore British access to the vast commercial wealth of Bengal ended in 1765 with the very real possibility that the Company had India within its grasp [*Doc. 7*]. In little under ten years, the East India Company went from being an important trader in the region to being responsible for revenue collection and civil administration of the whole of the Mughal provinces of Bengal, Bihar and Orissa. It proved to be much easier to build and maintain an empire from Bengal than it did from its possessions in the south, for not only could the British tap into the region's wealth, but they were more easily able to identify willing partners there. The buoyancy of the late Mughal economy was especially marked in Bengal, where a combination of location, rich natural resources, abundant labour and capital, and entrepreneurial zeal turned it into one of the wealthiest regions in India (Marshall, 1988). Much of that wealth was derived from overseas trade. By the mid-eighteenth century, goods from Bengal made up three-quarters of the Company's exports from India (Metcalf and Metcalf, 2002: 49–50). By way of contrast, the other two British administrations in India (or Presidencies as they were called at the time), Madras and Bombay, regularly ran deficits. Most importantly, the occupation of Bengal meant that the Company no longer needed to import bullion to pay for its commercial investments; instead these costs would be born by the land revenues it began to collect. By shifting their emphasis onto the collection of land revenues, the British were in fact emulating their Mughal predecessors who had also depended on such revenues to support their activities.

If events in northern India ultimately yielded much richer pickings than had been the case in the south, the root causes of British expansion were quite similar, for in Bengal the British were also acting in conjunction with other interests. Contemporaries would have seen them as just another group of opportunists operating within a very fluid and volatile environment. The situation changed dramatically in 1756 when Siraj-ad-daula (d.1757) was installed as Nawab of Bengal. While nominally accountable to the Mughal Emperor, the nawabs of Bengal had become largely autonomous. Siraj-ad-daula was the grandson of Alivardi Khan, who, as Nawab of Bengal from 1740 to 1756, had taken advantage of the growing commercial prosperity of the region to create a relatively stable and centralized administration, one which enjoyed considerable autonomy from the Mughal court while maintaining many of the outward signs of deference. Alivardi Khan's success was largely attributable to the adroitness with which he dealt with the competing interests within Bengal; his grandson lacked his tact and wisdom, though to be fair the pressures upon Siraj-ad-daula were much greater. In particular, Indian merchants and bankers were forging closer ties with the EIC in order to gain access to overseas trade.

Faced with a situation in which authority was slipping out of his hands, the nawab tried to restore control. His mistake, however, was in trying to impose it too quickly and simultaneously on several groups which effectively drove them into each other's arms. The crisis came in June 1756, only months after he had become nawab, when he dispatched a force to Calcutta to expel the British. The reasons for this action were relatively straightforward: EIC officials had erected fortifications against his direct orders. These fortifications were intended as a defence against a possible French attack, but Siraj-ad-daula concluded that they were a direct affront to his authority and a secure base from which he could be attacked in the future. His capture of Calcutta set in motion a series of events that not only ended with his downfall, but also prompted the British to take on a more aggressive role in order to protect their growing interests in Bengal. It also became the stuff of legends, for in the taking of the British fort at Calcutta a number of Britons were captured and imprisoned overnight. Conditions were such that many died, which proved to be a stroke of luck for British propagandists who embellished accounts of the Black Hole of Calcutta so as to depict the nawab as a cruel and heartless tyrant. Attention was diverted away from the reasons why the British were attacked and directed to the allegedly deliberate actions of a barbaric ruler. According to British accounts, 146 prisoners were thrown into a tiny airless cell, and only 23 survived. More credible sources not only put the numbers at 64 and 21, but also explain events not in terms of a deliberate act of cruelty but rather the unfortunate consequences of poor communications. The myth, however, proved to be more useful to the British [*Doc. 8*].

Given Bengal's commercial importance, the British were forced to respond quickly. The British knew that they could count upon support from the many merchants and bankers who depended upon the Company's trading activities, as well as from landed magnates who resented the nawab's efforts to curb their independence. In 1757 a force from Madras under Robert Clive was dispatched to recapture Calcutta. Clive has become a contentious figure in Indian and imperial historiography: to some he exemplified drive and determination; to others he personified corruption and naked self-interest. The nawab was not averse to the return of the British: he did, however, wish to contain their ambitions. But a conspiracy was hatched between the British and various vested interests in Bengal to topple the nawab and put a more pliant ruler in his place. The crisis culminated in 1757 at the Battle of Plassey, where a small British force was able to defeat the nawab who was fatally weakened by the refusal of many of his subordinates and their troops to take up arms in his defence. Plassey was not so much a stunning military victory as a hostile corporate takeover in which Indian agents played a critical role – bankers such as Jagath Seth and Omichand and the nawab's rivals such as Mir Jafar, who was later rewarded by being made nawab, eased the British into a position of dominance. The nawab's grandfather had warned of this possibility; his successor however was not so prescient [*Doc. 9*].

The immediate outcome of the Battle of Plassey not only re-established the British in Calcutta, but also enabled them to extract a number of privileges which would strengthen their position. Mir Jafar was forced to turn over land revenues to defray their military costs and he had to concede the freedom to trade without paying any of the local transit duties. The spoils of victory grew as the East India Company extorted from Mir Jafar monopoly rights over the trade in a number of profitable and strategic commodities, including salt and saltpetre. And it was not only the Company that benefited; private individuals gained from these transactions. Clive alone took away just under £300,000, including a personal *jagir* worth £28,000 given to him by Mir Jafar in 1759 (Metcalf and Metcalf, 2002: 53).

Mir Jafar, however, was unable to meet all these demands. He was replaced by Mir Kasim who the British thought would be a more effective administrator (d.1777). That he was, but not always in ways appreciated by the British as Mir Kasim was alive to the dangers posed by growing British influence and sought to contain them. Matters peaked in 1764 when Mir Kasim, in alliance with the neighbouring ruler of Awadh and the Mughal Emperor, met the British at the Battle of Buxar. Unlike Plassey, this was a real battle and the British came out of it as the major power in north India. The Treaty of Allahabad gave the British the office of *diwan*, or revenue collector, for the provinces of Bengal, Bihar and Orissa and in return the British acknowledged the titular sovereignty of the Mughal Emperor. Mir Jafar was restored but died soon after; he was succeeded by his son but because the British held the office of *diwan*, they effectively controlled the administration of the province. The nawab had become a hollow shell. Yet the return of the British to Bengal, even with their enhanced controls over the local economy and direct access to its revenues, did not yield the profits that had been anticipated. The British, working from the records of the old regime, over-estimated the revenue yields and ratcheted up the pressures on cultivators who also had to contend with a series of disastrous famines. The costs of containing conflicts elsewhere in India cut into their revenues and monies were still leaking into the hands of individuals.

CHAPTER THREE

CONQUEST AND CONSOLIDATION, 1765–1857

By 1765, British power was clearly in the ascendant. They had squeezed their French rivals from the south-east coast and had secured a firm footing in Bengal which gave them the promise of sufficient revenues to maintain their activities elsewhere in India. The grant of *diwani* to the British by the Mughal Emperor, who by this point was little more than a figurehead, had effectively confirmed their position. But being in the ascendant did not mean that they did not face challenges to their authority; much of India remained in the hands of ambitious rulers who struggled to carve out kingdoms for themselves and who resented British political and commercial intrusions, while within those territories that had fallen under their authority the British lacked the knowledge and the resources to impose their authority at will.

It is important to set these events within a wider global context. The loss of the American colonies in the 1770s and 1780s and the growing economic importance of Asia, when coupled to an intensification of European rivalries, first with France and later with Russia during the French Revolutionary and Napoleonic Wars, caused a strategic shift in British interests (Yapp, 1980; Ingram, 2001). Asia in general and the Indian Ocean in particular gained in importance and the British government became more interested in the activities of the EIC. Until 1858 the EIC remained nominally in charge of British interests in India, but it became increasingly subject to the scrutiny and control of Parliament (Lawson, 1993; Bowen, 1998). Accompanying this refocusing of political and strategic attention was the growing incorporation of India into a global economy, and increased exposure to the interests of western capital (Bose, 1990).

At this point, the British generally sought wherever possible to employ the administrative systems and procedures of the governments to which they had succeeded. For some, this blending of British and Indian forms and institutions was an ideal solution to a complex situation. Others, however, were not convinced, arguing that it was a marriage that frustrated genuine reform. This debate over the relative merits of trying to modernize and westernize Indian society through direct British rule and the application of British principles and practices, or proceeding more cautiously and hoping that the admixture of West and East would create the conditions for improvement, became a common feature in policy discussions right up until the British left in 1947. It would become caricatured as a debate between Anglicists and Orientalists respectively, though drawing a line between the rival schools of thought is actually much easier in principle than in practice (Bayly, 1988). Rather than treat them as discrete schools of thoughts, it is more useful to think of them as points along an ideological continuum.

BRITISH-INDIAN RELATIONS ON THE EVE OF CONQUEST

Before looking at the political and economic objectives and consequences of colonial rule in India, and the manner in which these unfolded, we should first take stock of some of the more general characteristics of the communities involved in these encounters. One of the first issues that needs to be addressed, given the degree to which colonial rule hinged upon Indian partnerships, is whether the presence or absence of what we would today call nationalism was a factor. We must first remember that few of the actors at the time had the benefit of hindsight, and in aligning themselves with the British most Indians could not have foreseen the consequences. It is anachronistic to speak of nationalism for it is a concept that only became common currency, in Europe as well as in India, towards the latter half of the nineteenth century. While there are certainly signs of patriotic attachment before then, the idea of the organic nation state to which we subscribe today was largely absent. This is not to say that there were no signs of wider political and cultural affiliations. Common cultural traditions and a sense of shared history helped to provide common reference points, especially in northern India or what was then known as Hindustan (Ray, 2002). However, these were not accompanied by durable political organizations that could mobilize and channel such identities. Hence, it is no surprise that the British never had to contend with a stable and coordinated India-wide alliance of Indian rulers. Deprived of the hindsight we enjoy today, Indian rulers were slow to realize the consequences of their growing entanglements with the Europeans.

Rajas and *zamindars* lacked a common class interest, traders and bankers were easily co-opted, and the peasants were denied an institutional focus around which to mobilize. Sikhs and Marathas had intense localized networks, but these were bounded by local religious and cultural idioms. This left the Mughal officer class or *mansabdars*, but the linkages between them had been weakened by colonial penetration. Mir Kasim is held out as a bit of an exception, both in his foresight and his strategic planning. Like many of his counterparts, he spoke a political language in which the British were identified as rebels and usurpers which does suggest that, at least on one level, the

British were viewed as alien and lacking legitimacy (Ray, 2002). Certainly, feelings against the British ran strong in some quarters, perhaps nowhere as strongly as with Tipu Sultan of Mysore. Among the items taken following the capture of his capital at Seringapatam in 1799 was a mechanical tiger (his symbol) which emitted a roaring sound as it simulated an attack on a prostrate sepoy dressed in the uniform of the East India Company. It is now on display in the Victoria & Albert Museum in London [plate 1]. That said, however, in the free-for-all that constituted contemporary politics in India, individuals scrambling for power took advantage of whatever alliances presented themselves, and from that perspective the EIC can be viewed as one of a number of competing interests.

The situation for many in Bengal (and elsewhere in India) is aptly captured in the Persian term *inqilab* which roughly translates as topsy-turvy (Ray, 2002). The world had indeed turned upside down. But for many there was no clear way forward. Instead, those whose ways of life were disturbed by the combined onslaught of colonial rule and the capitalist transformation of the economy often looked backwards, sometimes to an idealized past. But it would be a mistake to assume that Indian responses were instinctive and/ or merely reactive. There was considerable innovation and initiative within Indian society. Over time, nationalism began to emerge as individuals and groups, slowly and haphazardly in many cases, were drawn out of their local attachments to place or person and into wider networks of identity and loyalty. It was more commonly found in areas like Maharashtra and the Punjab. But even among the Marathas, this incipient sense of nationhood was all too often undermined by internal rivalries. In Bengal, where religious, caste and class affiliations proved more resilient, leadership was often provided by those Bengalis who, through western education, began to equip themselves with the vocabulary of political rights.

The structure and character of the British community in India, commonly referred to as Anglo-Indians, was also changing. What had largely been a small and self-contained society of traders and officials had grown as more officials as well as army personnel arrived in India. This in turn led to the growth of small European enclaves. Fort William at Calcutta, built between 1758 and 1773, was the largest British European-style citadel in India and Calcutta quickly became the focal point for Anglo-Indian society. Much of this can be attributed to it being the political and commercial capital of British India. Its growth attests to its role in the emerging empire; in 1710 there were between 10,000 and 12,000 inhabitants, by 1750 that number had reached just over 100,000, and it climbed to over 150,000 by the end of the century (Marshall, 2000). According to the 1839 census, Calcutta was home to 229,000 people (of which only a couple of thousand were Europeans).

The degree to which the British in India engaged with and even crossed over into Indian society has been the subject of considerable debate. This is especially true in the eighteenth century when the boundaries between the various communities appear, at least on first glance, as more fluid. For writers like William Dalrymple, the eighteenth century could almost be considered a golden age of cultural and social tolerance (Dalrymple, 2002). Others, however, such as P.J. Marshall, strike a more cautious note and emphasize the gulf which separated most Europeans from most Indians, except for under very controlled circumstances (Marshall, 2000). Between the two lie scholars such as Durba Ghosh who have complicated the discussion by emphasizing that the intensity and durability of cross-cultural contacts was very much conditioned by class. There was much more mixing, for example, among the lower classes in places like Calcutta (Ghosh, 2004) [see plate 2].

There were certainly a number of British officials who whether for personal or professional reasons established intimate relations with Indian society. A popular venue for interaction was the *nautch* dance: a form of public entertainment that combined Indian dancing and Indian music [see plate 3]. In the eighteenth century it was a popular form of recreation, but by the 1830s it was falling out of fashion, largely because Victorians were offended by Indian women dancing too provocatively. There are other examples of cultural interplay. Musical entertainments in late eighteenth- and early nineteenth-century British India were largely amateur in nature, heroic in their efforts, and occasionally multicultural in their output. Hindustani airs were transcribed and tablas and sitars occasionally joined harpsichord players (Woodfield, 2002).

The most convincing example of British intellectual and cultural engagement with India is to be found in the growing fascination with Hindu religious and philosophical writings. William Jones and Warren Hastings exemplify this curiosity (Franklin, 1995). William Jones was appointed to the Supreme Court in Calcutta in 1783 and arrived there having already studied Arabic and Persian. He helped establish the Asiatic Society of Bengal which provided a venue for the discussion of scholarly papers on a range of subjects pertaining to Indian customs and traditions (Kopf, 1969). Such oriental scholarship was marked by its preoccupation with ancient texts, and with the translating of such texts into English. Jones played a major role in such translations; upon arrival in India he began to study Sanskrit and he made what would become one of his most important contributions, identifying the close relationship between Sanskrit, Latin and Greek. Hastings promoted the study of Indian languages, and enthusiastically patronized Indian as well as European musicians and artists. Unusually for a governor-general, he was quite proficient in spoken and written Urdu.

Cultural contact was a two-way flow; most studies of orientalism have focused on the West's encounter with the East. But Indians also engaged with the British, both within India and in Britain itself. Thousands of Indians would travel to Britain, some driven by curiosity as to what they would find

there, others went to lobby the East India Company or the British government, deliver petitions or seek redress through the courts (Visram, 2002;
Fisher, 2004). But the vast majority went not by choice, but out of necessity.
Indian sailors or *lascars*, servants and nannies found their way to Britain.
Some stayed temporarily, others became permanent residents. Such a diverse
group not surprisingly experienced British society in quite different ways. But
for the most part, up until 1857 when the atmosphere became much more
racially charged, their experiences were determined more by their social
standing than by the colour of their skin. Wealthier Indian males married
British women, joined British clubs. One of the most famous of them, Dean
Mahomed, a Muslim aristocrat from Awadh, accompanied a British officer
back to Ireland, married a woman from a prominent Anglo-Irish family, and
then embarked upon several business ventures, including a restaurant and a
spa which were intended to satisfy a growing British curiosity with Indian
culture. In 1794 he published an account of his travels which counts as the
first published work in English by an Indian (Fisher, 1996). Another Indian
traveller who detailed his experiences was Mirza Abu Taleb Khan; his reflections following a visit to Britain and Europe at the end of the eighteenth
century are a fascinating example of how an educated and cultured Indian
evaluated and assessed western culture [*Doc. 10*]. What we find in their
accounts are very mixed views of British society. Some aspects of British life
impressed them, yet they were shocked by others. Given that most of the
surviving accounts were penned by men, there is a recurring fascination with
what they saw as the aggressiveness of British women. Much has been written of the often stereotyped accounts of eastern women by European males;
Indian males did much the same in their encounters with western women.

A further measure of the relatively more porous boundaries between
Indians and Britons is that persons of mixed ancestry in the eighteenth and
early nineteenth centuries did not experience the marginalization that would
be the fate of later generations of Eurasians. The most famous example here
is Lord Liverpool, who, as prime minister from 1812 to 1827, was one of
the longest serving prime ministers in British history. That his maternal
grandmother was Indian was not an issue at that time. This would not be the
case later when senior officials (though not the lower ranks) were specifically
enjoined against having sexual relations with Indian women (Peers, 1998).
To do so would be to risk one's career. By the middle decades of the nineteenth century, the Eurasian population of India was viewed with considerable
disdain by Anglo-Indians [*Doc. 11*].

INSTITUTIONS AND IDEOLOGIES OF THE RAJ

The revolution in Bengal hastened the transformation of the EIC from a trading corporation into a trading corporation with territorial responsibilities.

It was not a smooth or easy transition, and the EIC as well as the British government searched for a system of governance that would provide security, stability and a measure of accountability. Expectations had been high following the Battle of Plassey that the Company would soon earn windfall profits from its position in India, and would be able to transfer much of that wealth back to Britain (Bowen, 1991). In fact, by 1772 the EIC's ledgers were soaked in red ink and it needed government loans to keep it afloat. The price of Company stock had already fallen in 1769 when news of military setbacks and political scandals had reached Britain. Bankruptcy became a possibility. Efforts were made to discipline Company officials in India so as to reduce the corruption that threatened Britain's interests in India. For years after the Battle of Plassey, rumours circulated in London of the misbehaviour of Company officials in India. In Madras, for example, the attempts made by the newly appointed governor, Lord Pigot, to impose his authority over his council led to a coup in 1776 and his death following his imprisonment by the cabal ranged against him. Similar instances of indiscipline occurred in Bengal. One high ranking officer, General Richard Smith, gained notoriety in Britain and was the subject of a satirical play, *The Nabob*. Instances such as these illustrate the growing fear in Britain that if the activities of Company officials were to go unchecked the corruption would soon contaminate Britain.

We must first pause and consider the rather anomalous position of the Company in India. It did not enjoy sovereign authority, at least in legal terms, over the territories it administered. Instead, in Bengal it was acting on behalf of the Mughal Emperor who had granted it the rights of *diwani*. Elsewhere, the EIC was again often in the position of exercising delegated powers. This put the British government into an awkward position as well, for it could not claim sovereign authority over India. Yet it felt compelled to act owing to the growing public outcry. But it was reluctant to take on too direct a role (Sutherland, 1952). For one, it lacked the resources and knowledge to assume the Company's responsibilities. It was also wary of treading on the property rights of the Company; were it to abolish the Company, other chartered corporations, such as the City of London, would grow alarmed at the precedent. And finally the British government had to consider political opposition. The EIC enjoyed considerable political support in London, and any government which attacked the Company could expect fierce resistance in Parliament. Ultimately a compromise was reached whereby the Company retained its responsibilities for the day-to-day administration of its territories in India, but with greater parliamentary oversight.

The first foray in this direction came in 1773 with the passage of the Regulating Act. This piece of legislation was intended both to bring Company activities under parliamentary scrutiny and to set the foundations for a more effective bureaucracy in India. The awkward question of sovereignty was evaded: the Company was treated as enjoying *de facto* rather than *de jure* sovereignty. Under its terms, a governing council was established for each of the three Presidencies in India (Bengal, Madras and Bombay). This established a precedent by which the British government was to play an active role in designating the chief officials in India. By the terms of the Regulating Act, the governor of Bengal was also declared governor-general of India though there was little consideration of how to uphold his authority in practice. Coordination between the Presidencies became very difficult in such situations. A further problem emerged when it became clear that three of the four councillors dispatched to India were deeply antagonistic to the governor-general, Warren Hastings, and, because Hastings had a casting vote only in the case of a tie, until one of them died they consistently outvoted him.

Some of the shortcomings of the Act of 1773 were addressed in subsequent legislation, most notably in Pitt's India Act of 1784 which was intended in part to bring some order to the EIC's fractious councils in India. Out of it came an enhanced level of authority for the governor-general, in effect granting him extensive powers over his council and over the other Presidency governments in India. Such were the powers of the governor-general, that one would remark in 1849 that he and 'the emperor of Russia were the only two autocrats left in safety' (Baird, 1910: 59). In broader terms, this Act established a framework that would remain largely intact until the end of Company rule in 1858. It set the foundations for what would become known as dual government. The East India Company was made accountable to the British government. The British government had in practice the final say over all appointments to senior positions in India, which meant that governors and governors-general were often chosen on the basis of their political connections rather than their administrative acumen. Moreover, most were drawn from Britain's landed elite, thereby reinforcing the conservative tendencies within colonial rule (Metcalf, 1994). There were some exceptions; a number of governors and governors-general came to India with reputations as reformers (William Bentinck, Lord Dalhousie and Lord Ripon are perhaps the most famous examples of reform-minded rulers). The majority, however honest and incorruptible they were in their public conduct, tended to favour the status quo, and were instinctively hostile to social or political reform. Moreover, none were particularly intellectually gifted, and most were susceptible to the racial arrogance that became even more apparent in the aftermath of the revolt of 1857.

Another major event that would shape imperial attitudes in Britain was the attempted trial of Warren Hastings. It began in 1788 and lasted for seven years, ending in his acquittal in 1795 (Marshall, 1965). Orchestrated largely by Edmund Burke, but drawing support from others in the government, the charges that were drawn up against Warren Hastings were rooted in the accusation that he had acted cruelly, arbitrarily and without respect for the law [*Doc. 12*]. The trial exposed a growing difference of opinion between those who believed that public life should conform to universal standards, which was the basis of Burke's plea for justice, and those who defended Hastings on the grounds that he was acting in accordance with Indian custom and tradition. Burke was initially confident that his gambit might prove successful. Yet Hastings was eventually found innocent on all charges. This shift can partly be explained by a resurgent nationalism in Britain in consequence of the French Revolution. Hastings's repeated defence that he had acted to defend Britain's empire in a time of great vulnerability had a more receptive audience in 1795 than it might otherwise have had. Burke may have lost the impeachment, but he did manage to raise interest in India, and in so doing implant a sense of responsibility.

The trial of Warren Hastings signalled a growing engagement with India on the part of the British, not simply politically but also intellectually. The regular supply of news from India made it less remote to British audiences, and as these reports raised disturbing questions about British actions in India, more information was clearly needed. It became apparent that to administer India, the British required greater knowledge of the country, its people, resources and beliefs. Yet it would be a mistake to assume that knowledge was pursued only for practical reasons; increased British activities in India also stimulated a more detached curiosity about Indian culture and history (Bayly, 1996; Peers, 2005). The intensified search for information about India was driven by individuals as well as by the EIC, who came to appreciate how this information could make the task of administering India easier. So committed was the EIC that in the early nineteenth century it was spending more on science than was the British government (Drayton, 2000: 116).

The kinds of information that were being collected, analysed and disseminated ranged across the whole spectrum of intellectual life. Philologists tackled the origins and structure of Indian languages, in particular Sanskrit; botanists catalogued India's plant life; surgeons and physicians examined Hindu and Arab medical texts; antiquarians and later archaeologists probed the ruins of past empires in India; legal scholars consulted religious authorities and read the sacred texts to gain insight into pre-colonial relationships between law and society. By the end of the eighteenth century, not only had a great deal of information been collected but venues had been established for its circulation. Research societies began to appear in major cities in India, occasionally inviting Indians to join, and specialized journals were established to publish their research output (Kejariwal, 1988). Much of this scholarship was labelled 'orientalism' which, until recently, was understood rather benignly, referring simply to the study of the Orient, particularly through close reading of its texts, examining its monuments and studying its artefacts.

Since the publication of Edward Said's *Orientalism* in 1978, 'orientalism' has assumed a more malevolent definition as the knowledge that was being collected has been shown not only to be useful to colonial authority but also thoroughly implicated in it. This critique of orientalism was grounded in an appreciation that knowledge and power can never be separated and that knowledge is itself a manifestation of power. Bernard Cohn's work on the Indian census has shown, for example, that the data the British collected did not simply reflect Indian society but actually created categories to which Indian society was expected to conform (Cohn, 1996). A common characteristic of all these attempts to understand Indian society was their reliance on a series of essential truths about it, and in particular the determining power of religion (Inden, 1986). Hence, it is not surprising that, having credited religion with such authority, British officials would turn to religious texts to understand Indian society better. But while few would deny the importance of re-examining the assumptions which frame our understandings of India, cautions have been raised against the more extreme manifestations of post-colonial theory (Kennedy, 1996). The British did not by themselves construct India; much of their knowledge came from Indian intermediaries: the translators, interpreters, *pandits* and *maulvis* upon whom the British depended yet often failed to acknowledge (Bayly, 1996). Nor did this knowledge suddenly appear, willed into existence by an all-powerful colonial state. The census, for example, was not a wholly colonial invention: pre-colonial regimes also had to count and classify their subjects, often for the same reasons as the British, namely to tax and control them (Peabody, 2002).

IMPERIAL PRIORITIES: SECURITY, STABILITY, PROFITABILITY

Three objectives dominated British policy-making in India in this period (as well as thereafter): security, stability and the quest for profitability, or at least ensuring that there were adequate revenues to cover administrative costs. In achieving these objectives, the British undertook a number of policies that were to have profound effects on Indian society. To these a fourth objective can be added: social reform, though as noted earlier there was a paradox. The rhetoric of reform that began to percolate in the early nineteenth century can be misleading as not only did practice often diverge from principle, but also fear of the consequences as well as ongoing debates among policy-makers as to what should and could be achieved blunted many of the reformers' plans.

Uppermost for the British was the need to ensure the security of their footholds in India. While the conquest of Bengal had given them a secure bridgehead in northern India and the promise of a revenue base from which they could fund their activities, their overall position was far from guaranteed. Not only did they have to contend with challenges from still independent Indian states like Mysore, the Marathas, and eventually the Sikhs, all of whom were trying to extend their own empires, but there were anxieties as well about their neighbours to the north, west and east. They also had to factor in the very real possibility of internal challenges to their authority.

Moreover, the two were connected – British preoccupations with threats from outside India, whether they came from the French, Nepalese, Burmese, Afghans or the Russians, were predicated in part on the fear that should the British experience a setback on their outer frontiers then the shockwaves could incite internal revolt. The large armies raised by the British in India also worked indirectly to help secure the peace; many of the communities from which the British recruited were ones that had resisted British rule, and by employing what one British commander termed 'turbulent spirits', colonial armies acted as a sponge, siphoning off possible opponents. The predominance of Sikhs in the post-1857 army, far greater than their proportion of the Indian population would otherwise suggest, is partly accounted for by this, for the military conquest of the Punjab had come at great cost and with considerable difficulty.

Consequently, the British in India looked to their military forces as the ultimate guarantor of their security. A large standing army was raised, larger than most European armies, so as to deter attack from outside as well as provide internal security. By the early nineteenth century, the Indian Army had grown to nearly 200,000 troops, and to this could be added the 20,000-plus regular troops from Britain who were stationed in India. Thirty years later, the combined troops available to the British, comprising Indian sepoys and European soldiers, totalled more than 300,000, making it one of the largest standing armies in the world. Moreover, it did not cost British taxpayers anything and it could be used to bolster British interests elsewhere in Asia. Units were sent to Egypt in 1801, Java in 1814, and to China in the 1840s and 1850s. The Indian Army, financed completely out of Indian revenues, became an instrument for wider imperial goals, and is one of the better examples of how Indian taxes helped to subsidize British global interests (Peers, 1995).

The majority of the troops serving the British in India were locally raised, with the ratio of Indian troops to British troops in the period before 1857 varying between six and nine to one. But the officer corps from the 1780s onwards was exclusively British; earlier experiences had taught them that in the very fluid military labour market of India, Indian officers on occasion would switch their loyalties to whichever employer was willing to give them the greatest rewards, whether this consisted of more money, land grants, or enhanced status. Or they could try to use the troops under their command to carve out their own states. An example of this occurred in the 1760s when an Indian officer recruited by the British, Yusuf Khan, following his appointment as governor of Madura as a reward for his services, tried to establish his own kingdom, and when the British tried to reimpose their authority over him, he approached the French for assistance (Hill, 1914). This reluctance to employ Indians in positions of authority within the army was further bolstered by the growing racialist conviction that Indians lacked the right kind of character for command (Omissi, 1994).

In selecting Indian recruits for service in India, the British began by following Indian traditions, tapping into the pre-existing military labour market of India (Kolff, 1990; Alavi, 1995). In the north, certain rural high-caste communities dominated, such as Rajputs and Brahmins, while Muslims were prominent in the cavalry. Elsewhere in India, the Madras and Bombay governments drew from a wider spectrum of possible recruits, though neither government showed much inclination to recruit from the lowest castes. The prejudice towards high castes in the Bengal Army, and the degree to which the army not only tolerated but encouraged the observance of caste rituals, proved to be its undoing, for officers of the Bengal Army found themselves at the mercy of a remarkably homogenous and tightly-knit community, one which did not tolerate efforts at altering the terms under which it served. Sepoys were drawn to British service for a number of reasons; at least initially, the pay and allowances the British offered were greater than any of their competitors, and, perhaps even more importantly, the British quickly discovered that prompt payment of their sepoys was the surest way to secure their loyalty. Sepoys and their families could also look forward to pensions and preferential treatment in the courts and, for many, military service was not only customary but appealed to their sense of honour (Alavi, 1995).

The immediate threats with which the British had to contend in the years after the Battle of Buxar were located largely in southern and western India. Buxar had resulted in the British controlling Bengal and the neighbouring state of Awadh was reduced to dependant status. But in the south, the rising power of Mysore endangered Madras and outlying British posts while Maratha armies not only posed a threat to Bombay, but by roaming widely across Central India bumped up against the frontiers of Bengal and those of Britain's allies. If left unchecked, there was a risk that the Marathas could plunge India into chaos. As governor then governor-general (1772–85), Warren Hastings became convinced of the value of extending British influence through systems of alliances, striking a point midway between the Company's insistence on non-intervention and those officials who clamoured for conquest. All too often, however, such alliances proved to be unstable and short-lived. Not only was India's political landscape constantly shifting but British expectations of their allies were often unrealistic.

In 1778 officials in Bombay became embroiled in Maratha affairs when they aligned themselves with one of the claimants to the office of *peshwa*. Their efforts ended in a military debacle and Bengal had to commit extra resources to head off a coalition that threatened to pit not only the Marathas but also Mysore and Hyderabad against them. To make matters worse, there were signs of renewed French activity in India following France's decision to assist the Americans in their war of independence. The coalition, however, did not hold; by 1783 peace had been restored with the Marathas, thereby enabling the British to concentrate on containing the threat from Mysore which had grown more menacing with the arrival of French troops. Of the various powers ranged against them, Mysore was the most dangerous. Its armies had in the past laid waste to much of the Carnatic and by 1780 Mysore cavalry were at the gates of Madras.

The most ambitious plans to deal with Mysore and the Marathas came with the arrival in India of Richard Wellesley as governor-general. Precocious, impatient and ambitious, Wellesley was determined to make Britain the paramount power in India (Ingram, 1970). He rejected his predecessors' commitments to non-interference and instead took the position that Indian powers would either have to be conquered and annexed or forced into a position of subordination that would prevent them from challenging the British in the future. It was an audacious plan, and probably would not have secured support in London had Britain not been locked in a global struggle with France. By raising the spectre of French and later Russian interests at work in India, Wellesley ensured that India could be more easily drawn into Britain's strategic calculations. As this was a period of heightened patriotism, popular and parliamentary support for military actions could be counted upon. The extent to which Tipu Sultan had been demonized by the British press helped. Much was made in the British press of the horrific accounts of British captives being murdered, abused, and forced to convert to Islam, allegedly on the orders of Tipu Sultan (Colley, 2002). Plays and spectacles with Tipu Sultan featuring in them were still popular in London in the 1820s and he also crops up in the writings of Walter Scott, Charles Dickens, Wilkie Collins, Jules Verne and Captain Marryat.

Wellesley embarked on a multi-pronged strategy. First, he set out to strip Hyderabad of its French advisors and bring the state more firmly within the British orbit. Second, he planned a pre-emptive strike against Mysore where Tipu Sultan was in a precarious position. His animosity against the British had been stoked by the French; however, the French undercut his position by failing to provide any material support. Third, Wellesley set about reducing still further what little independence was enjoyed by the Nawab of Arcot and the king of Tanjavur in the south. They became little more than British client states. His fourth aim was to separate the Mughal Emperor from the Marathas and gain control over Delhi. Doing so would secure to the British the strategic heartland of north India, and also give them possession of the symbolic capital of India. The fifth plank of Wellesley's strategy was to secure India's north-west frontier against possible attack from either the Russians or the Russians in league with Central Asian powers (Ingram, 1992). This was the beginning of the so-called Great Game, which would last for over a century as the British tried to establish a secure and durable frontier to the north-west.

During Wellesley's nine years in India, the British finally defeated Tipu Sultan, which removed the one rival they had in the south, penetrated even deeper into Hyderabad and Awadh, took possession of Delhi, and gained greater control over the Carnatic and Tanjavur. In the Carnatic, Wellesley took advantage of the death of the nawab in 1801 to declare that the British would in future take sole charge of the administration of the territory. In so doing, one of the first examples of dual government was dismantled. The results of his campaigns against the Marathas were not as clear-cut; outright annexation was prevented by the strength of their resistance so he was forced to make do with a series of treaties that were intended to hobble the Marathas in the future (Cooper, 2003). That they failed to do so became evident in 1816 when the British were once again at war with the Marathas, though for the last time.

Subsidiary treaties like those used to try and control Hyderabad and the Maratha states are examples of another foundation of colonial authority in India, namely the policy of indirect rule. Rather than try to establish direct authority over the whole of India, which would be tremendously costly, not to mention politically contentious (Wellesley lived under constant threat of recall by the Company's directors), British strategy focused on establishing paramountcy under which Indian rulers were allowed to enjoy a quasi-independent status as long as they were willing to acknowledge British authority and did not disturb the peace. These arrangements routinely required that Indian rulers agreed to accept and pay for a detachment of Company troops, as well as host a British advisor or Resident. Not everyone, however, was as convinced as Wellesley of the utility of such arrangements. His younger brother (and future Duke of Wellington), who had commanded troops in the campaigns against the Marathas, doubted whether such treaties had much lasting power given what he saw as a fundamentally different concept of diplomatic relations in India [*Doc. 13*].

Princely states would eventually account for just over 40 per cent of the territory comprising present-day India, Pakistan and Bangladesh and contain about 20 per cent of the population. Many of these Indian princes found that what autonomy they allegedly enjoyed was under constant challenge as effective authority came to be exercised by the Resident. Many rulers chafed against these changes, petitioning for a restoration of their rights, others reacted more aggressively which usually resulted in the loss of their kingdoms. Still more succumbed to the loss of authority and prestige, sliding into decay, which ironically gave the British further grounds for intervention on the basis of bad government. Despite these challenges, a recent study has provided evidence that a number of princes proved to be effective rulers (Ramusack, 2004).

By 1820, the only surviving Indian state that could pose a serious challenge to the British was in the Punjab, where Ranjit Singh had built up a powerful army modelled along European lines (Major, 1996). He recognized the futility of going against the British and chose instead to expand in other directions, principally to the north and the west. Diplomacy, rather than force, was the preferred strategy in dealing with the Punjab, at least while Ranjit Singh was alive. His death in 1839, however, altered the equation and the British chose to respond in the 1840s to the civil wars that had broken out within the Punjab with a series of military campaigns that culminated in its conquest in 1848.

In adopting military action, the British were motivated by growing fears of Russian designs on Central Asia and India. As Russian influence penetrated more and more deeply into Central Asia, the British grew more determined to establish a secure and stable frontier so as to stave off any possible attack in the future. A decade earlier, the British had tried to intervene and impose a puppet ruler in Afghanistan – a decision that led to one of the costliest wars yet fought in India (Macrory, 1986). It was estimated to have cost upwards of £15 million, and taken the lives of 20,000 British and Indian soldiers and their camp followers. This quest for a stable frontier also led to the annexation of Sind in 1842 and another invasion of Afghanistan in 1878 (Khuhro, 2000). Cautionary voices were raised, however, about the seemingly inexorable pressures that playing the great game made upon the British, and that the quest for a stable frontier only served to draw them deeper into Central Asia [*Doc. 14*].

The security and stability of colonial rule did not depend simply upon military forces; the British looked as well to the introduction of a more efficient administration. Warren Hastings attempted with limited success to grapple with the task of separating the Company's territorial activities from its commercial operations. Moreover, he was expected to introduce much needed reforms into the operation of British rule in the province. The first of his priorities was to get rid of any remnants of effective Mughal authority. Yet he was just as convinced of the necessity of running the province using laws and policies with which the people would be familiar; to do otherwise was to risk an explosion. This helps to explain the persisting anomaly of the Mughal Emperor – the effective political authority of the emperors had long died out, but the British continued to maintain at least the outward fiction that they were ruling in his name until he was deposed and exiled in 1858 following the rebellion. The long-standing reluctance to allow British settlers into India was due to similar fears of upsetting the existing social order. Apprehensions that settlers would demand rights which might impinge on the Company, as well as lead to friction with Indians, persuaded the EIC, with the government's backing, to frustrate efforts to open India to British settlement. The fact that India had an abundance of labour and the high mortality and morbidity rates among Europeans served as further disincentives to potential emigrants from Britain. Concerns over how Indian society would respond to alien pressures also explains the prohibition against missionaries coming to India from Britain, which remained in place until 1813.

By virtue of assuming the *diwani* in 1765, the British inherited the responsibility for administering justice in Bengal, Bihar and Orissa. The legal system they adopted came into existence slowly and fitfully; pluralism was the

guiding principle, determined in part by pragmatism and partly by a preference for ruling people through what were believed to be institutions familiar
to them. Prior to 1858, legal procedures relied upon a complicated suite of
British, Hindu and Muslim laws and procedures. In general, Muslim law was
used in criminal cases, civil law employed either Hindu or Muslim law depending on the religion of the participants. Yet judicial procedures drew upon
British practices and punishments were modified to align them to British legal
custom. The legal system also took account of British priorities. Considerable
attention, for example, was directed at curbing what the British identified as
antisocial behaviour, including vagrancy and exhibiting bodily deformities.
Colonial law initially sought to avoid purely personal matters, and with it
domestic space. Consequently, households became an arena in which some
degree of autonomy from colonial rule could be asserted, which explains why
issues of gender and of the household would become so hotly contested.

The problem faced by the British was how to adapt a Mughal system,
which they understood only imperfectly, in such a way as to protect British
interests and facilitate commerce while not causing undue anxiety among the
wider population. In seeking to establish and authenticate Indian traditions
and practices, the British depended upon Indian translators and authorities,
preferring wherever possible to ground their actions on the basis of written
sources which could be explained to them by Hindu *pandits* and Muslim
*maulvi*s (Washbrook, 1981). By preferring ancient texts to actual custom and
tradition, the British not only strengthened the power of religion within civil
society but created opportunities for Indian experts to participate, albeit in a
supporting role, in the fashioning of the institutions and policies of colonial
governance. One of the most profound and long-lasting effects of the British
will to document and confirm traditional authority was the transformation
of caste from a cultural tradition into a legal taxonomy that fixed identities,
created rights and identified responsibilities. In this process, Brahmins played
a crucial role for they translated and interpreted many of the texts upon
which the British were so dependent. Not surprisingly, Brahmins were able to
capitalize on this dependency and they furnished the British with interpretations that bolstered their authority and status.

The role played by *pandits* and *maulvis* would, however, diminish over
time as British officials grew not only more confident in their knowledge of
Indian society but also came to be more and more convinced that tradition
was a barrier to material and moral progress. The 1830s, in particular, saw
a number of initiatives that signalled reduced dependency on traditional
authorities, most notably the declaration that Persian would no longer be an
official language. Indian scholars, who had hitherto relied upon their knowledge of Sanskrit and Persian to bolster their status, found that they no longer
enjoyed the same access to British power. Instead, it became clear that it was
those members of Indian society who had pursued western education who

were best positioned to act as mediators between Britain and India. This shift, however, was by no means complete or irreversible for a significant number of British officials still believed in the efficacy of what they identified as traditional authorities, including *pandits*, *maulvis* and Indian princes, and questioned whether western-educated Indians were sufficiently authentic and plugged into their communities.

The British also strove to ensure that the Indian economy would not only sustain their rule, but that there would be greater profitability in the future. Given the agrarian basis of the Indian economy, designing an efficient revenue system was uppermost in their planning. To reject Indian customs and impose their own methods was never a serious option for they lacked the local knowledge and resources to do so. The British tried to regularize where possible existing revenue systems so as to ensure a steady and predictable flow of funds to support their political and commercial activities. They chose to use pre-existing forms out of concern that to change things too quickly would not only threaten the revenues upon which they were depending (and in many cases had overestimated), but create resentments that would threaten their security. However, in so doing they all too often viewed Indian customs and traditions through western lenses (Bose, 1993). They believed that some reforms were needed, and that relations had to be standardized so as to ensure greater protection for property rights as a means of encouraging greater investment in land.

The British inherited a tax system in which the burden fell heaviest on the cultivators. One-third or more of the production was commonly claimed as the government's entitlement. These pre-colonial expectations became the Company's baseline. The British proved, however, to be more zealous in pursuit of these claims, and while in principle they were following their predecessors, in practice the actual amounts taken in were often greater. However, while it was assumed that one-third or thereabouts was standard across India, there were vast discrepancies across India as to the method through which such revenues were collected. The British were concerned to try and respect the balance of rights and obligations that were traditionally claimed by the actual cultivators and the various intermediaries who collected revenues on behalf of the state and who were entitled to a cut. However, fairness and equity were in the end much less important than stability and attentions concentrated on identifying those sectors of rural society which would best help to meet the twin demands of revenue and security.

In Bengal, attention focused on the *zamindars* who were viewed by the British as being the equivalent of European landlords, and, as we shall see, high hopes were entertained that these *zamindars* would provide rural leadership and furnish sufficient investment to enable economic growth (Guha, 1995). However, the actual power and influence of the *zamindars* differed as did their rights and perquisites. Some collected revenues from only a few villages and were not much better off than their neighbours; others were large territorial magnates, overseeing hundreds of villages and with bands of armed retainers numbering in the thousands (Marshall, 1988: 53–8). One of the largest *zamindar*s, the Raja of Burdwan, had 30,000 followers under arms. What they had in common, however, was that they were entitled to collect taxes and had an obligation to forward most of what they collected to the government. Legally, the British would come to treat them the same under the terms of the Permanent Settlement of 1793. The chief proponent of the Permanent Settlement was Lord Cornwallis, who had recently arrived in India to serve as governor-general. Influenced by his own aristocratic biases, Cornwallis strove to create an improving landlord class that would provide the political and economic security sought by the EIC. He insisted that 'A regular gradation of ranks . . . is nowhere more necessary than in this country for promoting order in civil society' (Marshall, 1988: 122). He believed that British principles, practices and personnel should be used wherever it was safe to do so, and where that was not possible, Indian forms should be adjusted to bring them in line. Further influences on the development of this policy can be traced to current economic theories which, having assumed that agriculture was the engine of economic development, emphasized the fixing of revenue demands so as to encourage growth (Guha, 1995). The introduction of the Permanent Settlement amounted to a tacit admission by the British that they lacked the wherewithal themselves to penetrate and control rural society and instead they hoped to employ the *zamindar*s as crucial intermediaries.

The principle which informed this legislation was that *zamindar*s would be given rights of ownership over their lands; in return, they would be expected to pay a set amount that was fixed in perpetuity. The hope was that not only would fixing the government demand encourage the *zamindar*s to increase output and bring more lands under cultivation, for they would be able to retain the profits accruing from enhanced production, but the land itself would become a marketable form of property that could be bought and sold or mortgaged. As for the peasantry, it was hoped that the *zamindar*s would recognize that it was not in their best interests to squeeze them too hard. Such expectations, however, were rarely met, and in many parts of Bengal, where the Permanent Settlement was in force, the peasants bore the brunt of the increased revenue expectations and there was little provision in the legislation to acknowledge and protect their customary rights (Bose, 1993). Nor did *zamindar*s fulfil the admittedly exaggerated expectations of them. Forced labour became more prevalent as cash crops were introduced to raise the revenues necessary to meet British demands. Commercialized agriculture was not new, but it penetrated deeper into local society and rendered it more vulnerable to outside forces. For example, when the prices paid for many of these cash crops crashed, many peasants were exposed to starvation. Indigo, one of the more common cash crops in this period, was especially volatile, with the prices paid for it varying by as much as 50 per cent in a single year. Further social dislocation was occasioned when many *zamindars* found that they were unable to meet the demands placed on them. By the terms of the Permanent Settlement, they were deprived of their lands. It has been estimated that up to one-third of the *zamindars* in Bengal defaulted and had their lands sold at auction (Tomlinson, 1993: 43). In some cases, this resulted in lands passing out of the hands of the traditional landed elite and into an emerging capitalist class. The EIC would later come to recognize that the Permanent Settlement had failed to match the expectations held of it.

These pressures on rural society compounded the damages that had already been done. Earlier efforts to increase revenue yields had coincided with a horrific famine that swept through Bengal in 1769–70, killing as many as 10 million or one-third of the population. Some recent recalculations suggest that the mortality rate might have been lower though the level of devastation still remains extremely high (Datta, 2000). All agree, however, that the Company did little to alleviate the crisis, whether through direct relief or lessening its revenue demands. So scarred was society by this famine that, a century later, it featured prominently in Bankimcandra Chatterji's novel, *Anandamath*, in which the famine was used to illustrate the cruel and destructive impact of colonial rule (Chatterji, 2005) [*Doc. 15*]. By the 1820s, revenues would become stabilized and the auctioning of *zamindari* lands had fallen off. But by then local economies had already become dislocated, societies had become unsettled, and rural violence was on the increase. There is also evidence to suggest that the structural transformation of rural Bengal fed into increased tensions between religious communities. Many of the peasants in Bengal were Muslim, their landlords Hindu. In other regions, Hindu peasants worked lands under the control of Muslim landlords. A revolt broke out in Bengal in 1831 under Titu Mir when Muslim cultivators killed a cow and splattered its blood on a temple erected by local *zamindars* (Bose, 1993: 148–51).

Zamindari was only one of a number of revenue settlements used by the British in India (Stein, 1992; Roy, 2000: 37–42). In southern India, officials like Thomas Munro championed a system that came to be known as *ryotwari* in which the state settled directly with the peasant cultivators or *ryots* (Stein, 1989). The political turbulence of the eighteenth century and the invasions by Haidar Ali and Tipu Sultan had prevented a well-entrenched class of *zamindars* from emerging in the south. Ideological arguments also came into play as Munro and others insisted that *zamindars* did not represent customary practice and that by settling directly with the peasants the British would not only be able to build a stronger and more flexible state but also ensure that the benefits of colonial rule reached right down to the level of the *ryot*. Advocates of *ryotwari*, like champions of *zamindari*, defended their plans by appealing to abstract principles. But they too were after much the same thing: increased revenue yields, and in the two-thirds of the Madras Presidency that fell under *ryotwari* system peasants were hard-pressed to meet demands placed on them. In the 1850s, a scandal ensued when it was discovered that Indian revenue agents were resorting to torture to meet the EIC's expectations (Peers, 1991). In other parts of India revenue settlements were made with village communities.

The degree to which colonial rule distorted or transformed the Indian economy is still a subject of intense debate. It is not so much a question of whether it changed, as the evidence is undeniable that it did so in dramatic if not necessarily intended ways, but whether such transformations were the direct consequences of colonial rule, or whether they were already under way and the results of a more general capitalist transformation of the world economy. A supplementary question that can also be asked is: if colonial rule is held to be accountable, to what extent was it deliberate? The debates over these questions have been raging for well over a century and show no signs of easing (Bose, 1990; Tomlinson, 1993; Roy, 2000). A number of dissenting voices were raised in Britain as to the adverse impact that British policies had upon India and particularly on the burdens being placed upon the peasantry. Similar concerns were voiced by Indian commentators; even those intellectuals and writers generally well disposed to British rule were quick to condemn its adverse effects on the Indian economy [*Doc. 16*]. Early nationalist icons like Romesh Chandra Dutt and Dadabhai Naoroji published books critical of British economic policy, focusing in particular on how the benefits of colonial rule were not shared equally. In what has become known as the drain theory, arguments have been advanced that there was a net outflow of wealth from India to Britain, owing to a combination of administrative charges levied on Indian revenues and the interest paid on loans raised by the British government in India that were used to undertake military operations and fund the building of an infrastructure that contemporaries argued were not always designed with Indian needs in mind. Critics of British policy also stressed the adverse effects of allowing British textiles to enter India at preferential duties, a policy which while benefiting British mills in Lancashire led to the serious erosion of India's domestic textile industry [see plate 4].

There are a number of indicators that confirm that the Indian economy was undergoing unsettling changes in this period. One of the most striking examples lies in the composition of Indian exports. In the mid-eighteenth century, Indian exports were dominated by fine textiles, finished cottons and silks bound for markets in Europe, Asia and Africa. By the second quarter of the nineteenth century, raw materials made up most of India's exports. Raw cotton rather than finished textiles, plus opium and indigo, and later tea, had become the principal exports. Beginning in the mid-1830s, British exports to India began to gain ground with entrepreneurs from Scotland and Lancashire leading the way. From the late eighteenth century, British mill owners had been lobbying the British government, initially to protect them from Indian imports and later to allow them access to Indian markets as their output surged. British textiles began to flood into India, which has led some historians to emphasize the role played by Indian markets in British industrialization. The value of British textile exports to India grew from £5.2 million in 1850 to £18.4 million in 1896 (Farnie, 1979: 33). The outbreak of the American Civil War marked another important stage, for the loss of American supplies of cotton forced British manufacturers to turn to India (Misra, 1999: 18). The price of Indian cotton quadrupled, encouraging cultivators to turn their fields over to cotton production. Yet the end of the war cut into the boom and prices for Indian cotton fell by a third after 1875.

India's integration into an emerging global economy is also evident in the growing trade between India and China. The EIC's monopoly, at least until 1834, extended as far as China where the EIC was under pressure to find commodities which they could exchange for Chinese tea, the demand for which was growing rapidly in Britain (Greenberg, 1969). Reluctant to ship bullion to China, the EIC looked first to cotton and later opium as the solution. Opium grown in India came to dominate this trade and the British used force to pry open Chinese markets. The Treaty of Nanking in 1842, which ended the First Opium War, that was imposed on the Chinese guaranteed British access to five Chinese ports as well as control over Hong Kong (Wong, 1998). Chinese apprehensions about the impact of opium, along with their anger at such blatant challenges to their sovereignty, led to further strife, culminating in the Second Opium War of 1856–60 which imposed still further demands on the Chinese to open themselves up to western traders. The willingness with which the British turned to the use of military force to compel Chinese consumers to accept a commodity which the British knew to have harmful effects can be accounted for in purely economic terms: by the second quarter of the nineteenth century, opium sales amounted to 40 per cent by value of India's exports (Washbrook, 1999: 403). The potential profits of tea exports to the United Kingdom and elsewhere in the British Empire led to experiments in growing it in India. The first tea plantation was established in 1830; by 1871 there were 295 in operation.

Another commodity that featured in British exports from India and which can also be linked to the destabilizing effects of colonial rule was indigo. Until its replacement in the late nineteenth century by artificial dyes, indigo was extensively used in dyeing cloth. It was a labour-intensive crop and, like tea but unlike other cash crops, it tended to be grown on large plantations under European supervision. It was subject to considerable price fluctuations, which rendered plantation labourers very vulnerable as their incomes often fell short of what they needed to purchase necessities. Relations on many of these plantations were extremely brutal and there was a constant risk of violence. Protests rocked a number of plantations in the 1860s (Kling,

1966). With memories still vivid of the Indian Rebellion of 1857–58, British officials in India, backed by a substantial segment of the Anglo-Indian community, cracked down on a British missionary who had translated into English a Bengali drama, *Nil Darpan*, which eloquently pleaded the case of the indigo cultivators [*Doc. 17*].

The growing commercial penetration of India led to demands for government investment in infrastructure; railways in particular were seen as a panacea to many of India's ills. Railways, it was expected, would open up Indian markets to British imports while simultaneously reducing the costs of getting Indian raw materials to the coast and from there to consumers around the globe (Kerr, 1995). Railway construction surged in the 1850s, largely as a result of the efforts by Lord Dalhousie who had arrived in India as governor-general in 1848. Dalhousie was not content to serve as a caretaker; he came to India convinced of the need to modernize the colony, and technology was one of the major planks to his plans. While the construction and operation of railways remained in private hands, the capital needed was only secured by the government providing guarantees on the investment. In 1849 Dalhousie arranged for a return of 6 per cent for British investors willing to invest in railway construction in India. After the Indian Rebellion construction took off, largely because the strategic value of railways in moving troops around India had been demonstrated. A total of 838 miles of track had been laid by 1860; the figure grew more than tenfold by 1880, and by the 1870s most major urban centres were connected to each other by rail. The construction of railways in India has long been heralded as an example of the beneficial results of colonial rule. Its proponents emphasize that railways stimulated India's export trade as well as linking together India's diverse communities. However, a cautionary note needs to be injected. The building of India's railways did little to stimulate heavy industry in India, at least at the outset, for the rolling stock and locomotives were imported from Britain. They were also paid for by the guarantees on Indian revenues to which the government agreed, and their routes were designed more with an eye to Britain's commercial and strategic interests than to the needs of the Indian economy.

The structural changes unleashed on the Indian economy by a combination of revenue demands and intensified commercialization had ramifications throughout Indian society. Competition from the cheaper machine-made textiles coming out of Britain led to the loss of important overseas as well as domestic markets for Indian producers, while the reduced number and diminished wealth of Indian courts limited their purchasing power. The standard picture, dating back to the nineteenth century, is that of a general de-industrialization of the Indian economy. Recent work, however, has shown that the situation was somewhat more complicated (Harnetty, 1991; Roy, 2000). Luxury production declined and the small Indian middle class often showed a preference for European fashions. But production for local markets continued, though it too faced competition, first from Britain and later from Japan and other industrializing countries. Together these helped bring about the decline of many traditional craft centres and large numbers of artisans were thrown out of work. The influx of British yarns also deprived many women of work for they had customarily played a major role in cotton spinning.

On the other hand, port cities like Bombay and Calcutta through which flowed raw materials destined for overseas markets grew in size and import- ance, while those individuals so positioned to capitalize on this trade also prospered. The transfer of power and wealth from declining groups to emerg- ing groups, with different tastes in many cases, led to a partial remapping of Indian society. While cities like Murshidabad and Allahabad which had hith- erto hosted aristocratic courts declined, there were those like Kanpur where sustained growth can be attributed to opportunities created by the colonial economy, in this case partly arising from the army's appetite for leather goods (Bayly, 1983). Indian entrepreneurs took advantage of the opportunities that were presented to them. Cotton mills were established around Bombay in 1853 and by 1880 there were 58 mills employing about 40,000 workers near Bombay and around Ahmadabad. Jute mills appeared in Calcutta in 1854 where jute fibres were used in making sacks, the demand for which soared with the surge in world trade. Most of the jute had hitherto been exported as raw fibres to mills in Britain, especially Dundee, and in Europe. But with the establishment of mills near Calcutta, much of the world's production came to be centred on Bengal. Whereas the cotton mills in western India were largely owned and operated by Indian entrepreneurs, many of them drawn from communities like the Parsis, the Baghdadi Jews or the Khojas, groups which historically had been active in international trade, the jute mills of Calcutta were dominated by Europeans. Yet even if Europeans came to dominate much of the manufacturing industries of eastern India, Indian merchants, especially ones drawn from the Marwari community that had spread into Bengal from its original homeland in Rajasthan, served as intermediaries. The fact that there were so few Indian entrepreneurs in Bengal (as compared to Bombay) has been explained by the fact that investing in land was more attractive than manufacturing. By the second half of the nineteenth century, being a *zamindar* involved less risk than being an industrialist, and it had the added advantage of offering a lifestyle more in keeping with traditional definitions of status and honour.

AN AGE OF REFORM?

In an earlier and somewhat more triumphant phase of Indian historiography, much was made of what has been termed an 'Age of Reform', a period lasting from roughly the 1820s to the 1850s that was marked by a growing intoler- ance of Indian customs and traditions and an optimistic faith that India could and should be modernized through the application of western practices and beliefs (Bearce, 1961). According to this perspective, British officials moved away from their earlier preoccupation with seeking stability by co-opting Indian institutions and individuals and instead they began to advocate large-scale reforms. Elements of this strategy have already been identified: the attempts to impose a modernizing class of landlords through the Permanent Settlement, efforts at encouraging the more rapid commercialization of Indian agriculture, and the first forays into reconciling Indian legal custom with British practice.

Proof of a more ambitious reform agenda has usually been traced back to the efforts made by the British to transform social practices and customs. There was certainly a lot of rhetoric at the time that implied such a shift, and the gestures that were being made reveal a more patronizing, if not downright negative, assessment of Indian society. Calls to allow Christian missionaries into India were growing and with them came heightened emphasis on west-ern education for it was felt that a combination of enlightened despotism, Christianity and western science would liberate India from the shackles of what was increasingly viewed as its oppressive past. James Mill, the noted political philosopher and historian of British India and a high-ranking EIC official, was one of the most strident critics of Indian society, and in his writ-ings and work at the EIC he sought to convince others of the need for reform [*Doc. 18*]. Governors-general like William Bentinck (1828–35) and Lord Dalhousie (1848–56) certainly committed themselves to improving Indian society: the former through his efforts to stamp out *sati* and *thagi* and his pro-motion of western education, the latter through his strategy of sweeping away the remaining Indian states and his encouragement of railways, telegraphs and irrigation schemes.

It is easy to exaggerate the much-touted efforts to reform Indian soci-ety by confusing rhetoric and practice. It was one thing to enact legislation against particular practices; it was quite a different matter to transform society so that it could incorporate the underlying values and principles. Traditions were not easily dislodged even with all the resources at Britain's disposal. A case in point is offered by the Widow Remarriage Act (1856) that was intended to provide a solution to the dire situations in which Hindu widows often found themselves following the deaths of their husbands. Indian custom had long discouraged the practice of widows remarrying; they were expected not only to remain faithful to their husbands long after they had died but also to live a life of poverty and self-denial. To do so not only brought honour to the family but also ensured that family property was not dispersed. This legislation was supposed to alleviate the impoverished condi-tions that widows faced by providing legal guarantees that, should they choose to remarry, they would not be deprived of any claims to their deceased husband's property. Yet this was not enough to overcome a long history of prejudice against widows. Legislation in fact achieved very little. A sustained campaign between 1881 and 1919 in Southern India led to only forty cases of Hindu women remarrying (Sarkar, 2001). More direct action was needed. The Bengali reformer Iswarchandra Vidyasagar, who worked tirelessly to encourage Hindu widows to remarry, often resorted to paying men out of his own pocket to marry them, but too often these men would soon after abandon their wives (Forbes, 1996: 20–3).

If its actual impact was less dramatic than its proponents and opponents claimed, the reform agenda nevertheless is an important signal of the directions which colonial rulers wished to pursue and thus is an indicator of the ideological and cultural changes that were under way. Moreover, as will be discussed in greater depth later, Indian society itself did not simply acquiesce to such reforms. Instead, these so-called reforms were debated and implemented within a context of Indian participation, though obviously most Indians did not and could not participate as equals.

Many of the most vocal critics of Indian society were Christian missionaries who, following their success in mobilizing the campaign against British participation in the slave trade, turned their attention to India. Until 1813, the British missionary presence in India was restricted by the Company's right to prohibit them from coming to India. Although the ban was lifted in 1813, and missionaries did become more active, a combination of Indian resistance and the Company's fear that their proselytizing efforts would antagonize local society meant that their freedom of operation was still constrained. The importance of Christian missionaries in forcing discussions on Indian social and cultural practices should not be underestimated; through their contacts with key British officials and their extensive networks back in Britain the British public was made aware of the Company's failure to encourage the spread of Christianity and Christian values, and pressure was brought to bear on British officials to address such evils.

At the same time, we must be careful not to exaggerate the direct impact of missionaries. Compared to other parts of the world where western missionaries were operating, they made relatively few converts in India, and of those, many were disparaged as rice Christians, the poor of India who missionaries suspected of having only converted as a way out of their crushing poverty. The individuals that missionaries most prized – the powerful, the wealthy and the influential – largely eluded them. But missionaries did have an impact on Hinduism, forcing Hindu spokesmen to argue for Hinduism in essentially western terms, and also encouraging some to look to western techniques to assist in the modernization of Hinduism (Jones, 1989). At the same time, the presence of Indian converts, while few in number, also helped to transform Christianity in India (Cox, 2002). A related question as far as the missionaries are concerned is that of their relationship to imperialism. Were they willing or unwilling accomplices as some would argue, a third column that helped facilitate colonial rule, or were they innocent of such charges? The most recent consensus would suggest that the truth lies somewhere in between and the relationship between their activities and the spread of imperial rule varied by time, place and individual (Porter, 2004). Some missionaries were eager proponents of direct British rule, believing that it would make their tasks easier. Others were publicly critical of imperial shortcomings.

One of the longer lasting contributions made by missionaries to the changing priorities of colonial rule was to focus attention on questions of domestic life in India, and in particular what was to western eyes the degraded condition of Indian womanhood. This marked a breach with the previous stance of the East India Company, which had, at least officially, taken a neutral position in terms of the private lives of its Indian subjects. Unless there was overwhelming evidence, drawn from authoritative texts, that demonstrated that social practices were in fact not justified, the British preferred not to meddle in domestic lives and arrangements. The reasons why gender would come to loom so large in British assessments of India are numerous, but include the fact that women were such a major force within the missionary movement and that the treatment of women had become a universal yardstick by which societies could be evaluated and ranked (Strobel, 1991; Cox, 2002). The Victorian preoccupation with bourgeois respectability and its attendant fixation on the appropriate treatment of women was exported to India where it provided a focal point for discussions about the state of Indian civilization.

The emphasis that was placed on questions of women's rights and their position within Indian society would in turn cause a backlash within it. Indian males, finding that their public status had diminished under colonial rule, often looked to the domestic sphere as an arena wherein they could reaffirm their authority. Attempts by educational reformers to extend western learning to Indian women were thus seen as a challenge to this authority – it is noteworthy that the University of Calcutta allowed women to graduate before its counterparts in Britain. Many of these intended social reforms were directed towards and felt more by upper- and middle-class women, for they were the ones who had access to education and for whom bourgeois notions of respectability and opportunity were not only attractive but also attainable. Colonial rule had a much different and less liberating effect on peasant women. With the growth of plantations and factories in which women were employed, many peasant women found their lives even more circumscribed as these new employment opportunities rarely came with any protection against economic or sexual exploitation (Sarkar, 2001).

Another factor that shaped British perceptions and reactions to Indian society during this period was the growing social and cultural gap between Britons and Indians. It would be an exaggeration to insist that relations in the eighteenth century had been completely open and marked by mutual respect, for in fact even those who were most curious about Indian society rarely doubted the superiority of the West. By the second decade of the nineteenth century, intolerance and exclusivity had become defining characteristics of British rule. Nor is there much evidence to show that apart from a few exceptional figures the British were particularly interested in or even aware of the culture surrounding them. British society in Calcutta was for the most part an insular community, one that deliberately kept its distance from its Indian neighbours by creating a largely self-contained community known as the 'White Town'. And as the numbers of Europeans in India grew, so too did their ability to create largely self-contained communities, ones in which the only regular contacts that Anglo-Indians had with Indians was with domestic servants or tradesmen, fleeting points of contact in which the difference in status most surely informed British reactions to Indian society. The number of servants which Europeans could expect to employ in India was staggering, far more than was common in Britain, and probably inflated their own sense of importance. For British women in India, however, this was offset by boredom and by the constant threat of death taking away themselves or their children [Doc. 19].

No doubt experiences and impressions such as these contributed to the hardening of attitudes towards Indian society. Whereas earlier generations had marvelled at the richness of the Indian past, by the 1820s the focus was on the stagnancy of the Indian present. What had once been romanticized as proof of the timelessness of Indian society came increasingly to be seen as an obstacle to progress. Early attempts at understanding Indian society had made much of the fact that villages seemed to be largely self-contained and governed by rituals that ensured social harmony (but the reality was quite different – villages had long been integrated into sophisticated long-distance trading networks). A number of theories to explain this alleged stagnation entered circulation. The effects of climate were often used, especially in describing Bengal (Harrison, 1999) [Doc. 20]. What we would today label as racialist thinking also came into play, with comparisons being drawn between Indians and other inferior 'races'. But it would be a mistake to assume that there was a consensus over such questions. The concept of race was itself too slippery to make much sense of, and there were observers who found aspects of Indian society worth admiring (if not necessarily worth imitating).

The abolition of *sati*, or the practice whereby widows would commit themselves to the funeral pyres of their deceased husbands, has long been held up as an example of a social reform aggressively pursued by the British. In fact, while the practice of *sati* was not that widespread (though there was some evidence that it was on the increase) it came to exert a powerful influence on the British as it symbolized for them the barbaric and superstitious nature of Indian society. In 1823, for example, it was estimated that there were 575 *sati*s in Bengal (Hamilton, 1828). By the early nineteenth century, the treatment of women had become one of the most common indicators of social development. Hence, much more attention was paid to *sati* than might otherwise have been the case and more discussion was centred on *sati* than on many of the larger problems facing Indian society, such as the famines and epidemics that resulted in many more deaths.

The British response to *sati* exposes one of the paradoxes of colonial rule. While *sati* became a crucial site upon which the merits of western society could be displayed, the Company's commitment to working within the boundaries of Indian tradition forced it to devise a strategy to stamp out the practice but only by working within an identifiable Indian tradition. Textual support for abolition was needed, and so the battle between reformers and their opponents took place over competing interpretations of religious texts. The British elicited the support of Indian authorities to bolster their case. Of these, the most famous was Rammohun Roy. He provided arguments in support of abolition by disproving claims that *sati* was in fact a recognized and sacred Hindu rite [*Doc. 21*]. In addition, fear of the potentially explosive consequences of treading too harshly on Indian traditions persuaded the governor-general, William Bentinck, to canvass all regimental commanders as to whether they were at all apprehensive that abolition could cause unrest within the ranks of their regiments (Peers, 1995). These regiments, recruited largely from the higher castes, had become bastions of a Hindu orthodoxy, and the British, far from wanting to undermine the status of their recruits, were keen to nurture it, feeling that it produced better soldiers.

Recent scholarship has shifted the focus away from the familiar juxt-aposition of tradition versus modernity and instead looked at how the figure of the *sati* was used to articulate different visions of patriarchal authority (Mani, 1998). The intensity of the debates between reformers eager to abolish the practice and its proponents who defended it in terms of religious orthodoxy was less about the actual sufferings of, or the religious actions taken by, women and instead was rooted in the question of who had the right to speak on behalf of women (for women themselves were not consulted). In fact, even British views of *sati*, while horrified at what they thought was a barbaric practice, were informed by an almost grudging admiration for the image of female sacrifice. Painters such as William Hodges, who personally observed a *sati*, wrote of the solemnity and dignity of the occasion and composed his painting accordingly [see plate 5].

The British obsession with *sati* was paralleled by their fascination with *thagi*, or the ritualized murders of travellers, ostensibly to appease the Hindu goddess Kali. Like *sati*, *thagi* was held up as proof of the debased nature of Indian society. There was one critical difference, however, and that was that the numbers of persons affected by *thagi* were considerably greater though equally difficult to specify with any degree of accuracy given that many of these murders took place in areas remote from British authority. Reports of *thagi*, like *sati*, captured British imaginations and they both featured in artistic and literary works [see plate 6]. Meadows Taylor's *Confessions of a Thug* was a best-seller, with Queen Victoria being one of its biggest fans.

The identification of the *thagi* problem, and the subsequent campaign to eradicate the gangs of thugs believed to be roaming about northern and central India, was occasioned by reports in the 1820s and 1830s that increasing numbers of travellers were being robbed and murdered, apparently through a ritualized form of strangulation [*Doc. 22*]. Until 1830 *thagi* was treated as a political and legal problem, but it would become a moral issue around 1830 owing to the convergence of a greater commitment to reforming India as well as the skill with which William Sleeman, who was tasked with the suppression of *thagi*, was able to convince authorities that thugs were not simply robbers and therefore could not be dealt with by simple policing measures (Woerkens, 2002). Instead, Sleeman emphasized that this was a community tied together by religion and fiercely committed to a ritual from which they could not be easily dissuaded. Proof of this was offered by thugs having their own distinctive language and vocabulary, which Sleeman would later compile into a dictionary.

It is difficult to define with precision who exactly were the thugs owing to the extent to which subsequent efforts at identifying them have had to operate within the framework imposed by Sleeman. While religion probably played a role, it would be a mistake to view them as yet another manifestation of barbaric Hindu religious practices, if for no other reason than the fact that many of the captured thugs were Muslim. Nor can they easily be romanticized into social bandits as it appears that the looting they did was only to benefit themselves. Probably the best way to define them is as predatory entrepreneurs who took to robbing travellers because they had the opportunity to do so. The years when the thugs were most active happened to be the same years when much of Central India was undergoing considerable stress on account of the break-up of the Maratha confederacy and the tentative beginnings of colonial rule. Large numbers of soldiers who had previously served in the armies of the various Maratha warlords had been disbanded, and in the absence of other alternatives it is not surprising that many took to robbery.

However, the British viewed *thagi* as distinct from highway robbery, and even though there was no evidence to demonstrate that such attacks were becoming more common, their need to establish their authority made it incumbent on them to respond. This they did by defining these attacks as rooted in something uniquely and particularly Indian. Because thugs were thought to be criminal because of their birth, they could not be dealt with through normal legal channels. They were criminal by virtue of their identity as thugs, and hence guilty by association. This made prosecuting them easier; all that was needed was to establish that they were thugs. Moreover, as their guilt was attributed to cultural failings, rather than individual culpability, they had to be collectively re-educated and reformed. This combination of ethnographic classification and extra-legal measures to deal with a crime that could not be accounted for easily within western legal traditions would lay the foundations for what became known as the Criminal Tribes Act, legislation that was introduced in the 1870s which effectively criminalized whole communities and then sought to control them through measures similar to those developed for use on the thugs (Nigam, 1990; Singha, 1998).

The other major initiative undertaken by the British during this period which has been singled out as proof of a reforming agenda was the government's commitment to the introduction of western science and education. A close examination of the debates within official circles reveals that there were few who challenged the superiority of western education. While vestiges remained of the earlier orientalist fascination with ancient Indian philosophy and literature, western education was deemed necessary to modernize India. Discussions turned around what was the best means to implant western learning in India and to that end the question became what was the best medium of instruction (Zastoupil and Moir, 1999). Earlier claims in favour of trying to educate as far as possible through the use of vernacular languages, as advocated by James Mill and others, and which were intended to help disseminate western learning as widely as possible, came under increasing attack in the 1830s. Thomas Babington Macaulay, sent to India to serve as the law member of the Governor-General's Council, issued a vigorous rebuttal to such claims, insisting that a genuine transformation of Indian society could only be achieved through the use of English-language instruction [*Doc. 23*]. Only then could the British be assured that they were nurturing the kind of improving spirit within India that was necessary.

Given this emphasis on educating the elite rather than the masses, and the restricted resources made available for education, the impact of these early educational policies was very limited. Western education affected only a tiny proportion of the Indian population and even then it was largely confined to the major urban centres. Even after 1857, when government investment in higher education grew, expenditure on primary education remained largely static. Yet the impact of these policies cannot be measured simply by looking at the numbers affected. In the same year that Macaulay issued his infamous *Minute on Indian Education*, the government declared that from that time forward English was to be the official language of the government. Government employment thereafter depended upon competence in the English language and therefore there was even greater pressure on the Indian intelligentsia, particularly those referred to collectively as the *bhadralok*, to become familiar with western science and literature. By 1835, the Calcutta Book Society had sold 31,864 books in English as compared to 3,384 in Hindustani, 36 in Arabic and 16 in Sanskrit (Chaudhury, 2001).

The combined impact of these policies, while not affecting the vast majority of the people in India, was felt by two groups in particular. Muslim elites, who had sought to retain under the British the positions they had enjoyed under the Mughals and their successor states, found it increasingly difficult to do so as Persian was no longer in demand. In many parts of India, Muslim intellectual activity turned inward. Upper-caste Hindus, however, proved to be more receptive and, through their participation in western education, they not only secured government employment, but were introduced to a political vocabulary which they could later use to criticize colonial rule for its short-comings. The ironic legacy left by Macaulay and others was that the policies which they promoted resulted in the creation of a community which the British would later come to despise and fear. The *babu*, a term of derision for the western-educated Bengali, who was intended to serve as an instrument through which India could be reformed and modernized, would come instead to be regarded as untrustworthy and insufficiently authentic.

INDIAN REACTIONS AND INITIATIVES

Efforts made by historians to assess how segments of Indian society responded to the challenges of alien rule have had to contend with a number of difficulties, not the least of which is the absence of Indian voices in many of the surviving records. Setting that aside, we must still contend with the fact that it is difficult to generalize about Indian responses owing to the fact that not only were a variety attempted, but Indians themselves were not simply reacting to colonial pressures, and in many instances they were trying to take the initiative and impose their own meanings and attempting to control the forces of change around them. At the same time, one can identify a number of patterns which help to make sense of the diverse reactions and responses to colonial rule that have been observed. One way of conceptualizing these responses is to locate them along a spectrum ranging from acculturation to accommodation and then on to avoidance and resistance, including what James Scott has aptly termed 'everyday weapons of the weak' (Scott, 1985). It is, however, important to note that individuals and groups were not limited to one style of response. They would often experiment with different types, even at the same time, in their efforts to control and understand the changes happening around them.

As already noted, the imposition and maintenance of colonial rule was dependent upon the assistance given by key sectors of Indian society, if not enthusiastically and willingly, then at least tacitly. There were any number of reasons for Indians to choose the path of accommodation. To describe such individuals as collaborators, given the pejorative meanings we now associate with that term, is not particularly helpful, for it implies that they were acting out of self-interest when in fact their actions stemmed from a diverse and sometimes contradictory range of calculations and assumptions. As we have already observed about the eighteenth century, Indian rulers often struck alliances with Europeans after having calculated that it would give them a strategic edge over their rivals. Over time they would find themselves increasingly dependent upon their European partners, but by then it would be too late and hence many had to cooperate with the British so as to ensure their survival. Accommodation was for many the only alternative, especially as they lacked the kind of political vocabulary that would have enabled them to undertake a coordinated response on an India-wide basis (Ray, 1998: 519–20). Accommodation also took place at other levels of Indian society. Merchants who depended upon access to European markets and bankers who looked to the EIC as an investment figure here. So too did the sepoys who joined the Indian Army. As we have already seen, not only did military service provide an income, it also provided status and an occupation with which many were already familiar.

There were others who were drawn to the British out of expectations that through contact with western ideas, practices and customs, Indian society could be regenerated. Acculturation refers to the conscious and unconscious acceptance of new ideas, often with the intention of revitalizing Indian cultural practices and institutions. Yet many who chose this path would find that no matter how much they integrated western ways, they would never be treated as equals. Nor did such individuals merely ape western ways. A study of the emergence of a politicized middle class in Lucknow shows that while its emphasis on respectability smacks of Victorianism, it did not simply mimic developments in Britain but drew on local cultural dynamics (Joshi, 2002).

Much of what could pass as acculturation took place in major urban centres like Calcutta, Bombay and Madras. Calcutta was the political and commercial centre of British rule in India from the 1760s through to the end of the 1800s and consequently Indians who resided there experienced the most sustained and intimate contact with the British. Bengal's banking, intellectual and commercial elites assumed early on a special authority as representatives of Indian opinion and aspirations. And as we have already seen, the British were often dependent upon their expertise, local contacts and capital. But over time Indian financiers and capitalists became increasingly marginalized, squeezed out by British competitors in centres like Calcutta and Madras though they fared somewhat better in Bombay (Misra, 1999).

A striking example of acculturation is offered by Rammohun Roy who founded the Brahmo Samaj ('Truth Society') in 1828 in an effort to blend European rational enquiry and the political ideals of liberalism with the wisdom of Hinduism, which had for him become corrupted and encrusted over the centuries (Jones, 1989). He was the son of a prosperous *zamindar* in Burdwan district, Bengal, and in his youth learned Persian, Sanskrit and Arabic. He proved to be an adept businessman, using the monies gained from lands inherited from his father to become involved in the commercial life of Calcutta. Politically he was drawn to liberal ideals of free trade, freedom of the press, individualism and rational enquiry, and was instrumental in launching several of the first Persian and Bengali newspapers in India. In 1803 he published a book which was very critical of the practice of worshipping images and enjoined his readers to adopt monotheism. He believed that there are some truths common to all religions, but that all of the world's major religions, including Christianity as well as Hinduism, had become encumbered with superstitious rites and questionable dogmas, and set out to return Hinduism to the pure forms he found expressed in the most ancient Hindu texts, the Vedas [*Doc. 24*]. In 1818–20 he had joined the debate over *sati* by publicly demonstrating that it was not sanctified by ancient Sanskrit texts. Roy has been idealized by some, demonized by others. To the former he was 'the father of modern India'. Others have questioned his impact, seeing him as atypical and having limited relevance to the broader changes occurring within India. And then there were other religious authorities in India who argued that he had a faulty appreciation of ancient Hinduism, and as such not only did he betray his birthright but also played into western attacks on Hinduism. One such figure was Dayananda Saraswati, the founder of a later reform movement, the Arya Samaj (to be discussed in the next chapter) [see *Doc. 25*].

Moving further along the spectrum of possible responses we come to avoidance, or the attempt to lessen colonialism's impact by limiting as much as possible contacts with it, both mental and physical. Avoidance often manifested itself in expressions of nostalgia – a wish to turn the clock back and return to an earlier, perhaps imaginary, golden age. Frequently, this led to battles over what was tradition and who had the right to define it. As has been pointed out, 'It was precisely because the assault of Western modernity was so fierce that large areas of Indian society came to reject it and to promote counter-ideologies premised on the self-conscious defence of tenaciously held "traditions"' (Washbrook, 1999: 397). But, as the quotation marks around 'traditions' suggest, we cannot take such 'traditions' at face value. Rather, many of these so-called 'traditions' were only just being defined, and the process by which they came into being relied upon a degree of British-Indian interaction that was more complicated than a simple model of British domination and Indian resistance allows.

Many of the strategies of resistance that could be counted as ones of avoidance can be found within the responses by the Muslim community to colonial rule. This is not intended to typecast a diverse community, for one can find plenty of examples of Muslims pursuing different strategies. There were frequent occurrences of armed confrontation in which Muslims featured, the example of Titu Mir's revolt in Bengal having already been noted. And as we shall see in the following chapter, the Aligarh movement spearheaded by Syed Ahmed Khan in the aftermath of the Indian Rebellion sought ways of reconciling western science and education with Muslim values and tradition. But as a group, Muslims had collectively experienced relatively greater erosion in status and authority with the break-up of the Mughal Empire and the slow decline of many of the major urban centres with which they had been associated (Robinson, 2000). The cultural and intellectual vitality in cities like Lucknow, Delhi, Murshidabad and Allahabad had suffered in the transition to colonial rule (Bayly, 1983; Hasan, 2005).

By the mid-nineteenth century, Muslims accounted for about one-quarter of the population under British rule. A far from homogenous community, events over the course of that century would encourage greater convergence among them, at least as far as a sense of collective identity is concerned. Some were migrants from Central Asia and beyond, but most were local converts. However, they were not evenly spread across India. Nor were they contained within any specific social strata. Large concentrations could be found in the north-west (in what is today Pakistan) and in Bengal in the north-east and, as already noted, many of the latter were poor cultivators. Elsewhere in India, the Gangetic heartland for example, Muslims had historically occupied socially and politically important positions and they were the ones who had to contend with the deterioration in their status and influence. Not surprisingly, many were eager to restore Islam to its previous glory, and reformers like Sayyid Ahmad Barelvi (1786–1831) drew large crowds in the 1820s. What is notable about his efforts and others like him was how little influenced by western ideas were their plans of regeneration (Metcalf and Metcalf, 2002: 84–5). Instead, they looked within the history of Islam for guidance.

The most spectacular responses to colonial rule, though not always particularly effective, were acts of resistance. These took many forms, from the kinds of state-organized campaigns of the Marathas and other communities to individual acts of defiance which may consist of little more than a symbolic challenge to colonial rule. Yet we should not dismiss such incidents, for however trivial they might appear, they do provide a window into the experiences and attitudes of those living under colonial rule (Guha, 1983; Hardiman, 1992). Acts of vandalism, when looked at in the aggregate, can reveal patterns that are indicative of popular consciousness; a good number, for example, were directed at telegraph poles and railway tracks, often the most obvious symbols of colonial authority in rural areas. In 1829, at the British garrison at Meerut, near Delhi, local villagers protested against what they saw as the desecration of their space by the British. The body of a British soldier, who had been tried and executed for murdering his sergeant, had been hung in chains at the outskirts of the base as a way of setting an example to his colleagues. Local farmers, upset at this invasion of what they considered to be properly their space, retaliated by cutting down the body in the middle of the night and dragging it back into the centre of the camp.

Larger and more violent confrontations were also quite common in this period and we have already seen examples of this in Titu Mir's revolt in Bengal and in the indigo protests of the 1860s. Another case in point is offered by the Santal revolts of the 1850s. The Santals, who occupied marginal forested lands in eastern Bengal, found themselves increasingly penned in as agriculturalists and timber merchants pushed their way onto their lands. In the 1840s the British tried to stabilize the region by settling the Santals into a large reserve. This was part of a wider process undertaken by the British to bring tribal societies under tighter control so as to improve agricultural productivity and increase tax yields. A charismatic leader known as Siddhu appeared in 1855 who urged them to strike back at the moneylenders and the British officials who symbolized the threat to their autonomy. The army was deployed to put down the revolt, causing considerable loss of life, but this took place at the same time as the British were also trying to assist the Santals to settle into their new lands. Contemporary observers, such as W.W. Hunter who would later include these struggles in his ethnography of rural Bengal, were not without sympathy for the Santals, though their comments betray a romanticized and sentimentalized appreciation of what they would have understood to be a doomed and primitive culture [*Doc. 26*].

Between the extremes of collective mobilization and individual defiance lies a grey area where it is often difficult to differentiate between social protest and criminality. Of interest here is what the British referred to as *dacoity*, which roughly translates as gang robbery or brigandage. To the British, it was proof of the lawless nature of Indian society, yet, as researchers have found, there is a correlation between the level of *dacoity* and the kinds of pressures with which rural societies had to cope (Arnold, 1986). There may not have been an explicitly political agenda which underscored bandit activity, but the fact that so many took to *dacoity* is indicative of the level of turmoil within rural societies. It tended to become more frequent during periods of famine, and many of the captured *dacoits* turned out to be individuals who had lost their land, their employment or their status during the upheavals that marked the first century of colonial rule. Discharged soldiers, for example, took to *dacoity* in many instances though, as recent research suggests, not necessarily in response to poverty. They looked to it instead as a means of reclaiming their status as warriors or sometimes as a way of settling a grievance (Downs, 2002).

CHAPTER FOUR

REBELLION AND RECONSTRUCTION, 1857–85

THE INDIAN REBELLION, 1857–58

By far the most dramatic expression of Indian discontent with colonial rule came in 1857–58 when much of northern India was rocked by a series of mutinies and popular revolts which would eventually convulse most of the central Gangetic Plain and reach down into Central India. For several months in mid- to late-1857, the very survival of British rule in India was in doubt, and when the magnitude of the crisis became known in Britain in the summer of 1857, one popular magazine captured the anxious mood when it wrote: 'Our house in India is on fire. We are not insured. To lose that house would be to lose power, prestige, and character – to descend in the rank of nations, and take a position more in accordance with our size on the map of Europe than with the greatness of our past glory and present ambition' (*Illustrated London News*, 4 July 1857). The rebels, whether they were sepoys, peasants or *taluqdars*, also quickly appreciated the significance of these events or what they termed the 'devil's wind'. The actual cost in human lives will never be known with any certainty. It has been roughly estimated that 6,000 of the approximately 40,000 Europeans then in India were killed. The number of Indians who died during the mutiny and the famines and epidemics that followed in its wake is far more difficult to compute. Attempts to do so based on comparisons between the very sketchy demographic data that we have for the period before 1857 with the census results of 1871 have suggested that the number of deaths might be around 800,000. It could well be higher than that. In addition, the revolt led to tremendous property destruction and caused the government of India's debt to jump from £60 million to £100 million. Not surprisingly, the increased burden of debt financing was borne by Indian revenues. More alarmingly, however, the war quickly took on the attributes of a race war, one in which intensified racial and religious animosities caused participants on all sides to commit atrocities against each other.

While the last remnants of the revolt would be quashed by early 1859, battles continue to rage among historians who are still trying to come to grips with what was not only a dramatically charged episode, one which had long-term repercussions on the people of India, not to mention on relations between Britain and India, but was also a remarkably complex sequence of events which defy easy analysis. The fact that historians cannot even agree on what to call this period in Indian history is proof of these challenges. Some prefer to call it the Indian Mutiny, a term which, while acknowledging that it was the sepoys in the army of the Bengal Presidency that first rose up, does not do justice to the level of popular participation in the ensuing struggles. At the opposite extreme are those who have labelled it a war of independence, a title which more cautious historians question as implying a greater degree of cohesion and forethought than much of the evidence suggests. By titling it a rebellion, I wish to avoid these two extremes and instead draw attention to the diverse reasons why it occurred and the various motives of those who participated, before going on to look at its consequences. The actual course of events has been ably documented elsewhere and for the most part is not contentious (David, 2002).

The difficulties we face in reaching a consensus on the origins of the Indian Rebellion as well as what it meant to those who participated in it should come as no surprise for contemporaries were often equally baffled, though no less fascinated with what had taken place. It led to a huge spike in interest in Britain in what was happening in India, and with that came a wider debate over Britain's position in and responsibilities to India. This growing awareness of India also took more imaginative forms. At least a hundred novels on the Indian Rebellion were produced between 1857 and 1964, and a number of the British officers who served there, such as Henry Havelock and Henry Lawrence, would become stock heroes for generations to come. In trying therefore to make sense of 1857–58, we are faced with the challenge of digging our way through the many levels of impressions and understandings that have been built up over the years. An excellent example of this lies in the front matter to what has become one of the classic Victorian histories of the rebellion, J.W. Kaye and G.B. Malleson, *The Indian Mutiny of 1857* (4th edn, 1891), an important source for historians today. Kaye was the original author but died before he could complete the work; Malleson then took over. In his preface, Kaye had written, 'The story of the Indian mutiny of 1857, is the most signal illustration of our great national character ever yet recorded in the annals of our country. It was the vehement self-assertion of the Englishman that produced this conflagration, it was the same vehement self-assertion that enabled him, by God's blessing, to trample it out'. Malleson's preface shifts attention towards the differences between Indians and Britons, and illustrates how the idea of race had gained greater currency in the years after 1857: 'Proud of being an Englishman, I desire to place on a record that shall be permanent the great deeds of my countrymen. Lord Beaconsfield never wrote more truly than when he said that everything depends on race . . . the race which inhabits this isle has known how to triumph, not only unaided, but when heavily handicapped by fortune'.

While the events of 1857–58 were not completely unforeseen, for Lord Dalhousie had prophetically mused in 1848 that 'In India one is always sitting on a volcano', the sheer magnitude of the military and civilian uprisings came as a great shock (Baird, 1910: 24). All this begs the question of how a state which was so thoroughly saturated with military values, and where military needs took priority, could fall victim to an uprising. Were they caught napping, and if so, why? In fact, the imperial early warning system had registered signs of discontent for some time. There were a number of British officers who had grown convinced that mutiny was a very real possibility and tried to awaken their colleagues to this threat. Signs of discontent within the Bengal Army had been multiplying for the past decade as sepoys grew disillusioned with their terms of service. Their rates of pay had not changed for decades, the extra pay and allowances that were given to those who volunteered for service outside the boundaries of the Presidency had been withdrawn, and a new enlistment act of 1856 now obliged them to serve wherever they were sent. There is also evidence that officers were becoming more distant from their men for the growth of the Anglo-Indian community in India, even in isolated cantonments, provided officers with more opportunities to detach themselves from their Indian surroundings. In common with many British civilians in India, officers in the Indian Army were becoming more contemptuous of India and more convinced of their own superiority (Metcalf, 1994).

Much has been made of the fact that just prior to the outbreak of the rebellion sepoys were given a new rifle which required them to use cartridges that were rumoured to be greased in cow or pig fat. These cartridges had to be bitten before loading, thereby offending the religious sensibilities of Hindu and Muslim sepoys by threatening them with ritual pollution. But the fact that rebels were often quite willing to use these cartridges when firing on their officers indicates that the significance of the cartridge issue can be easily overblown, and that in fact it was little more than a catalyst, though the reactions these cartridges caused among the sepoys is suggestive of deeper causes. In particular, it points to the sepoys' alarm at what they feared to be a growing disinclination on the part of the British to respect their customs and traditions, and it was an anxiety which they shared with many other Indians who were also increasingly angry at the changes happening around them. And therein lies part of the answer as to why the revolts of 1857–58 drew their support not only from the military, but also from the peasantry as well as the elites in many parts of northern India, an area which, compared with Bengal or Madras, had not had as long a period to adjust to the new realities of colonial rule [*Doc. 27*].

A number of explanations present themselves which together help account for popular unrest. British rule was increasingly viewed as more aggressively alien by many Indians. Christian missionaries had become more active in northern India which fed fears that Indian religious practices were under threat. British actions like the introduction of the Widow Remarriage Act (noted previously) fuelled these suspicions. The effects of land revenue settlements also need to be factored in, for not only did the overall demand grow, which hit many hard, but the increased commercialization of the Indian economy had benefited some at the expense of others. Those *zamindars* and *taluqdars* who had lost out under British rule often joined the rebels as a means to re-establish their wealth and status while those who had gained either assisted the British or remained neutral (Stokes, 1978). Indian elites were also becoming more disillusioned with British rule. What many viewed as arrogance and a lack of respect for their customary rights was dramatically confirmed for them when Lord Dalhousie introduced his doctrine of lapse. In his rush to modernize India, Dalhousie had embarked on an ambitious plan of annexing the territories of Indian princes for he believed that princely states were one of the major obstacles to Indian improvement. Conscious, however, of the need at least to appear to be operating within the confines of the law, Dalhousie introduced a policy whereby those Indian states which did not have a direct male successor would lapse to the British. Indian custom had hitherto allowed its rulers the option of adopting or designating an heir apparent; in the late 1840s there were a number of Indian states where the successor had been adopted and these were now taken over by the British. Those who had been dispossessed of their titles and their livelihood would become magnets of disaffection and would provide the rebellion with a number of its leaders. The annexation of Awadh in 1856 would prove to be especially unsettling (Mukherjee, 1984). Justified on the grounds of chronic Indian misrule rather than taken over through the doctrine of lapse, British rule in Awadh threatened many of the landed magnates there who had hitherto enjoyed considerable autonomy. British rule brought with it a more aggressive land revenue settlement that deprived many of the existing *taluqdars* of their lands and villages. Many of them rose in revolt and they were joined by many peasants. And as Awadh was the homeland of the majority of the sepoys in the Indian Army, any threat to the status or livelihood of their families weakened their discipline and loyalty, and helped to forge closer links between the mutinying sepoys and the civilian rebels.

The first signs of insubordination were detected in the sepoy lines at the cantonment of Barrackpore in January 1857 and reached a crescendo in the six months between May and November 1857 when, following a mutiny of troops at the British base at Meerut (one of the largest in north India), the sepoy deserters then fell on Delhi, which they captured. Near simultaneous mutinies broke out elsewhere in the cantonments of the Bengal Army and by the end of June much of the territory between Delhi to the west and Lucknow to the east was in rebel hands, for the sepoys had been joined by peasants and *zamindar*s who also harboured grievances against the British (Mukherjee, 1984; Stokes, 1986). Revolts also broke out in Central India where sepoys joined local magnates and peasants in the territory around Jhansi and Gwalior. There is no one date at which the rebellion can be said to have ended, for pockets of resistance existed until the spring of 1859. But the final relief of Lucknow in March 1858 largely confirmed the re-establishment of British authority.

Delhi was the symbolic epicentre of the revolt for it had long been the capital of the Mughal Empire, and one of the first things that the rebels did was declare that Bahadur Shah, the Mughal Emperor who was living on a British pension, was the emperor of Hindustan. It is clear that Bahadur Shah was a most reluctant leader, and in fact had little choice for he was the virtual prisoner of the rebels. But he proved to be a potent figurehead, and the rebels who streamed into Delhi following the uprising at Meerut and other encampments drew considerable support from the population at large who harboured a number of grievances against the British. Ironically, while the possession of Delhi enhanced the credibility of the rebels, it also proved to be a tactical misstep for it allowed the British to concentrate their forces, drawn from eastern Bengal and the Punjab, on the city. Rather than spreading outwards and carrying revolt further afield, the rebels were instead besieged within the city. Beginning in June 1857, British forces, including a large contingent of Sikhs, began to gather on the ridge to the north of the walled city, and in September, following the destruction of one of the city's main gates, they recaptured the city with much loss of life and a great deal of looting. Bahadur Shah would be the last of the Mughal Emperors; captured following the siege, he would spend the rest of his life in exile in Rangoon. His sons and successors were executed by the British officer who captured them.

Kanpur would become another focal point in the Indian Rebellion. There, the British confronted a rebel army which had been raised by Nana Sahib, the adopted son of the last of the *peshwa*s, who, after unsuccessfully trying to persuade Dalhousie to maintain his pensions and perquisites, tried to restore Maratha authority. Mutinous troops were joined by peasants and small landlords who were suffering under the new revenue settlements imposed by the British. The siege began on 6 June 1857 and ended with the infamous massacres at the end of that month. On 26 June, the garrison, realizing just how hopeless was its position, surrendered after receiving promises that their lives would be spared. Shortly after boarding boats for the trip down the river, rebels on the river banks opened fire and most of the troops were killed. Soon after, some two hundred women and children – who had been left behind following a promise that they would not be harmed – were murdered and their bodies tossed down a well. The legacy of these events should not be underestimated for the well became for the British the ultimate symbol of the rebellion. Their soldiers were no longer simply fighting to uphold British rule; they were also fighting to avenge the deaths of British women and children.

It is not clear who gave the fateful order that led to the murder of the women and children. Contemporaries were quick to blame the two leaders, Nana Sahib and Tantia Topi; more recent studies, however, have concluded that it was not planned and was more the result of a demand for vengeance on the part of people in the mob who had by now heard stories of the arbitrary executions and other brutalities being committed by the British force that had been sent to relieve the British garrison (Mukherjee, 1990). The British relieving force arrived a day after the women and children had been murdered. It was commanded by General Neill, unhinged at the best of times, who was seized by a pathological fury which spread to others. Garnet Wolseley, then a young officer serving with the 90th regiment, declared in a letter home that 'my sword is thirsty for the blood of these cursed women slayers' (Kochanski, 2000: 17). Wolseley also reported that when his unit captured a rebel who was subsequently sentenced to be hanged, every man in the regiment volunteered to be the hangman. Normally, this was a task which soldiers did their best to avoid. A sergeant at Dinapur wrote home that 'the men are mad, and oh, how they go about swearing and vowing to avenge this atrocity. They are wrought up to the highest pitch of madness, and are burning to go at these murdering monsters' (Malcolm, 1891: 101–02).

The events at Kanpur lent credibility to the many rumours in circulation of British women and children being raped and murdered, and contributed to the growing demands for revenge and retribution that were being made in Britain as well as in India [*Doc. 28*]. But British investigators would find no proof that British women or children had in fact been raped. Yet the readiness with which these rumours were believed even after they had been disproved goes to show just how powerful a force gender had become in differentiating between civilized and uncivilized peoples (Paxton, 1998). By accusing the rebels of perpetrating such acts against women and children, who had become for the British the ultimate symbols of civilization, the British were not only able to justify immediate acts of retribution but also became more convinced of the importance of race and the extent to which they were superior [see plate 7].

As the one-time capital of Awadh, Lucknow had long been associated with the Muslim rulers of north India, and attracted rebels seeking to restore the old order. Quickly encircled by rebel forces containing disbanded sepoys along with discontented peasants and *taluqdar*s, the British Resident, Henry Lawrence, fell back with a small number of loyal sepoys on the British Residency. The siege of the Residency began on 1 July, and on 25 July General Havelock set off from Kanpur to try and relieve the garrison holed up in the Residency. His force managed to punch its way through the 42 miles between Kanpur and Lucknow, but was so strained by the fighting that it had to fall back on Kanpur to regain its strength. Another push began on 19 September. After three battles, Havelock's force found itself in Lucknow on 25 September but did not have sufficient strength to provide cover for the garrison to withdraw, and soon found itself under siege. Despite this setback, the situation for the British was improving. While the symbolic value attached to the defence and eventual relief of the Lucknow Residency is undeniable, these battles were in fact diversions from the main operations which were taking place along the Ganges. In commemoration of the siege, the Union Jack flew day and night over the ruined Residency until the last moments of British rule in 1947 [see plate 8]. Delhi had been retaken, giving the British control over a place of great strategic and symbolic importance. The British would finally retake Lucknow for good in the spring of 1858.

The major centres of revolt in Central India were the small state of Jhansi and the historic fortress of Gwalior, home to Maharaja Jayaji Rao Scindia, and capital of one of the last surviving Maratha states. The lapse of Jhansi to the British triggered what can best be described as a popular revolt, with cultivators joining rebel troops in acts of violence against the British. The outbreak of mutinies among troops garrisoning Gwalior was a major setback for the British, for not only was Gwalior one of the strongest fortresses in Central India but its pro-British ruler was viewed by the British as characterizing the kind of modernizing prince that they hoped others would emulate. The Rani of Jhansi drew considerable support from the people at large, and with the arrival of Tantia Topi, the two joined forces and fought a number of actions against British forces who were rushed into the area. The Rani fought at the head of her troops, falling in a battle outside Gwalior in June 1858. The Rani of Jhansi came to occupy a prominent place within the Indian nationalist pantheon, symbolizing not simply resistance but also such feminine virtues as self-sacrifice, for she fought and died on behalf of her adopted son. Her sacrifice offered parallels to medieval bardic traditions that celebrated Rajput women who took their own life by committing *sati* rather than be captured and dishonoured by the enemy. It is therefore not surprising that women who joined the Japanese-sponsored Indian National Army in the Second World War were formed into a brigade named after the Rani of Jhansi, and her image continues to be celebrated in popular art where she has come to exemplify Hindu beliefs in the power of the goddess figure or *shakti*.

With the benefit of hindsight, it is clear that what assisted the British in their suppression of the rebellion was the degree to which it remained largely confined to the Gangetic Plain of northern India and that there was no overarching plan to coordinate the rebels' activities. The rebels may have shared a number of similar grievances, but the objectives they pursued were often quite different. For some of the leaders, it was the restoration of their traditional authority, others fought to reclaim lands that had been lost to them, for others the fear that their religions and customs were under threat was an undoubted motivation, while many of the rebels probably joined in because of the temptations offered by the state of lawlessness. There was no single vision beyond that of confronting colonial rule. Much of southern and western India remained quiet, which not only reduced the threat from those quarters but also allowed the British to redeploy troops to where they were most needed. Equally important was that the Punjab, only recently conquered, did not break out in revolt. Instead, the British were able to raise troops there to help fight the rebels. There was no shortage of volunteers as many Sikhs were eager to avenge themselves on the sepoys of the Bengal Army who had only recently conquered and humiliated them. And finally the British were blessed with a bit of luck as a large contingent of troops from Britain bound for service in China were diverted to India.

LEGACIES OF THE REBELLION

Memories of 1857–58 were seared into the collective consciousness of Indians and Britons alike. The violence that marked this conflict left a legacy of mistrust and apprehensions which would inform later British policies as well as shape Indian responses to colonial rule. Hindu rebels had been polluted with cows' flesh before being hanged or blown from the mouths of guns. Muslims were hanged in pigs' skins or forced to chew on pig fat before execution. Thousands of prisoners were hanged from trees in the *doab*, often on the flimsiest of evidence. The growing estrangement between Indians and the British, which has already been noted, was exacerbated in the climate of fear and anger. British behaviour in India changed as racist attitudes became more prevalent, as did acts of individual violence committed against Indians. Government officials complained of what they saw as an alarming increase in the disrespect in which Indians were held as well as more frequent instances of Indians being publicly assaulted [*Doc. 29*].

Not all British officials succumbed to the pressure for vengeance. Cooler heads did occasionally prevail, but those officials who championed restraint were often abused for being soft on the rebels. The governor-general at the time, Charles Canning, was heavily criticized when he tried to re-establish the rule of law by insisting that guilt must first be established before Indians could be punished. Consequently, he was reviled in the press and given the nickname 'Clemency Canning'. Indians in turn were shocked by many of the atrocities committed by British troops, with many of the victims having had nothing to do with the revolts. Not all Indians rebelled against the British; many remained loyal or at least stayed out of the conflict. And the British depended on a larger number of Indian troops to assist in suppressing the rebellion than their accounts might otherwise suggest. There were some exceptions: the crucial contributions made by Sikh soldiers from the Punjab

would be acknowledged in their being given preferential access to the recon-
structed Indian Army. Indians from the *bhadralok*, who had come to identify,
at least in part, with western education and western ideologies, grew alarmed
at the increasing tendency of the British to view all Indians with hostility and
suspicion. Many of the rebel leaders would in turn become nationalist icons
in the twentieth century.

Someone had to take the blame for such a costly and major embarrassment as the rebellion. A scapegoat was needed and the one closest to hand
was the East India Company. In some respects, its days were already num-
bered for not only had it lost all of its commercial functions but it was
increasingly subject to parliamentary scrutiny. British manufacturing interests were becoming ever more vocal in their condemnation of the Company,
and what they claimed was its failure to facilitate their growing commercial penetration of India. Missionaries lobbied against what they saw as
the Company's lack of enthusiasm for their efforts to convert Indians to
Christianity. Even before the rebellion there was a growing chorus in Britain
pressing for direct British rule.

In 1858, the odd convention of the British ruling India through a
commercial corporation which was also legally the subject of the Mughal
Emperor came to an end. No longer was India administered by an independent corporation beholden to shareholders, subject to parliamentary oversight,
but also drawing its claims to sovereignty from rights given to it by the
Mughal Emperor. The winding up of the EIC, the banishment of the Mughal
Emperor, Bahadur Shah, and the murder of his heirs by the British officer
who had captured them saw to that. It is, however, misleading to assume that
there was a complete transformation of British policy in India. The potency
of the Mughal Emperor would remain as the British sought to incorporate
Mughal symbols into their political actions and public architecture. Extensively choreographed ceremonial functions such as *darbar*s drew upon British
readings of Mughal symbolism. Similarly, imperial architecture shifted away
from the neo-classical forms imported from Europe and looked instead to a
hybrid style known as Indo-Saracenic that fused together Gothic, Persian and
Rajput styles (Metcalf, 1989). Most of the personnel and much of the bureau-
cratic practices that had been developed by the EIC remained in place.
However, the end of Company rule rendered India more susceptible to the
scrutiny of Parliament, and, by extension, to the British public. There was no
longer an intermediary to act as a buffer. This is not to say that India suddenly
became a central issue in British political life. Indian topics, like many imperial issues, only occasionally aroused parliamentary interest. India did become
a more regular feature in British media, but this was as much due to advances
in communications and the rapid growth in the number of newspapers and
their readers as it was to the ending of the East India Company. Yet in doing
away with the EIC, India was brought more closely within Britain's orbit.

Not surprisingly, even before the violence had subsided, the British began to search for explanations. Some looked solely to the army, and by treating the rebellion as almost exclusively the result of a breakdown of discipline in the Bengal Army, focused their attention on ensuring that this would not happen again. The high-caste sepoys of the Bengal Army were largely blamed, and it was decided that the British in India should never again place themselves in such a position of dependency. Nor should they allow themselves to be so outnumbered, and so one of the first actions after 1858 was to reorganize and restructure the Bengal Army. They shifted their recruiting efforts away from Awadh and its high-caste recruits in favour of the Punjab where Sikhs and Muslims had proved their loyalty. Ironically, though one of the lessons learned in the rebellion had been to ensure that no one group dominated the army, recruits from the Punjab would over time do just that (Omissi, 1994). That they were able to do so came about largely because of a growing conviction on the part of the British that individual communities in India had unique aptitudes: those from the Punjab were deemed to be martial races and so were thought to be ideally suited to military service. The declaration that Punjabi Sikhs and Muslims, as well as Gurkhas, were martial races is an example of the growing commitment to what can be termed colonial ethnography, which resulted in an intensified effort to classify Indians into discrete communities. It was also decided that the number of British troops in India had to be permanently increased so as to reduce the ratio of sepoys to Europeans to something more like three to one rather than the five or more to one that had previously been the norm.

While most observers were unwilling at this time to consider that the rebellion commanded widespread popular support, they did concede that it consisted of more than discontented soldiers. In particular, they noted that the rebels looked towards India's traditional elites for leadership and from that deduced that one of the sources of the revolt lay with the numbers of *zamindars* and princes who had become alienated from British rule. There was also a consensus that fears that Indian religions were under threat had driven many to rebel. Coupled to this was the belief that in many instances the more easily-tricked Hindus were seduced into rebellion by scheming Muslims, with the former acting out of fear for their religion and the latter by a desire to restore their authority. It was argued that the British had made a mistake in trying to reform Indian society too quickly, and that the modernizing strategies associated with Bentinck and Dalhousie were partly to blame, for no matter how well-intentioned such measures had been, Indian society was just not ready for them [*Doc. 30*].

The outbreak of the rebellion was also seen as an embarrassing intelligence failure and hence the British sought to rebuild links with those groups in society thought to be the most authentic expressions of traditional authority. It was argued that the British had to move more cautiously and to try and rule India through those individuals who were identified as India's traditional leaders. Like many observers, Benjamin Disraeli, who would shortly become prime minister of Britain, was convinced that 'respect for the military power controlled by socially conservative territorial aristocrats was fundamental to India's peaceful governance' (Klein, 2000: 562). This marked a striking reversal from the previous decade when Dalhousie had successfully argued for the need to rid India of the last vestiges of native authority. The Star of India, an honorific award given enthusiastic backing from Queen Victoria and Prince Albert, was instituted to reward those princes who had remained loyal or at least neutral during the recent conflict. It was hoped that this would help stabilize rural society in India by acknowledging and bolstering the authority of traditional magnates. A more tangible demonstration of this renewed engagement with the landed classes of India can be seen in Awadh. The 1856 settlement in Awadh, which had curtailed the privileges enjoyed by the *taluqdar*s in favour of granting more rights to the cultivators, was overturned and many of the *taluqdar*s, provided they were willing to submit themselves to British authority, were reinstated and most of their lands returned to them (Metcalf, 1964).

The apogee of this revived conservatism, one that was heavily tinged with a romanticized view of Britain's place in India, came with the 1877 *Darbar*. It was intended publicly to acknowledge and celebrate the decision in Britain to give to Queen Victoria the title of Empress of India. For Victoria and the prime minister at the time, Benjamin Disraeli, it was an opportunity to bolster their popularity by tightening their association with India. Yet what was missed by many contemporaries, eager to cut Disraeli down to size, was that Queen Victoria was the driving force. She saw herself as Empress of India, and would take this role very seriously in the future. Osborne House, her summer residence on the Isle of Wight, featured an Indian *darbar* room, a *munshi* or Indian scholar was kept on her staff, and Indian regiments were given prominence in the parades held to commemorate her 1887 and 1897 jubilees. For the Viceroy, Lord Lytton, the *darbar* was an occasion at which Indian nationalists could be overawed with the might of the British Empire [*Doc. 31*]. Lytton, one of the most romantically inclined Viceroys sent to India, was determined to mount an elaborate show and imaginations ran riot.

The end result was a weird marriage of Gothic romanticism and orientalism, or as one wag has put it, Agra Saxon. Princes and rural magnates from across India, other members of the Indian elite, and numerous British officials and military units converged on Delhi where the *darbar* had been organized in such a way as to display the hierarchies of British India (Trevithick, 1990). Delhi had been chosen because it was a traditional imperial capital as well as the epicentre of the Indian Rebellion: the *darbar* was intended to be a dramatic statement that Britain had inherited the imperial responsibilities of its predecessors. Those attending the *darbar* had their positions on the ground carefully plotted so as to indicate clearly where they stood with reference to the centre of power: the Viceroy. It was a massive undertaking with nearly one hundred villages being cleared to create the site. Yet it was visually jarring for many, a pastiche of Indian and British images and symbols jumbled together. At times it verged on becoming a theatre of the absurd. One officer, who obviously had not done well on his language courses, declared to his troops, 'Pigs, you now have a cat to wear around your neck'. The designers of the *darbar* also failed to take into account Indian sensibilities: the medallions of the Queen, for example, which were widely distributed, were viewed as blasphemous by many Muslims. Moreover, there is the obvious paradox of an event that was intended to frame British rule in terms of the past glories of a faded Mughal Empire and the use of the Queen as a symbol of a modern western society.

The most contentious aspect of the 1877 *Darbar*, however, was that such a large and expensive undertaking took place at a time when a devastating famine was sweeping through much of south and central India [*Doc. 32*]. Millions were dying at the same time as the spectacle was being mounted. It has been estimated that the 1876–78 famine affected some 36 million people and caused the deaths of upwards of 4 million (Kumar, 1983: 231). The famine, followed by the excesses of Lord Lytton's *darbar* and the expenses of the Second Afghan War which broke out at this time, provoked a heated debate back in the United Kingdom which was at least partly responsible for Disraeli's defeat in the election of 1880. Nevertheless, the *darbar* would remain a fixture of British rule and several more would be held.

If the post-1858 mood among British officials leaned in favour of a more cautious and conservative ideology, one which rested upon the belief that Indian society was not ready for the kinds of massive changes that earlier reformers had advocated, it did not completely tilt in that direction for there remained a commitment that the institutions and policies of colonial rule would have to be modernized, which when combined with increased commercial activity would hopefully produce long-term improvements. Moreover, enough remained of the pledge to pursue liberal policies to ensure that some vestiges of the earlier rhetoric of reform remained, albeit constrained by security fears. The end result, as one historian has put it, was that India became a 'laboratory for the creation of a liberal administrative state' (Metcalf, 1994: 29).

This commitment, at least on a rhetorical level, was signalled by the terms of the Queen's proclamation of 1858 that heralded the end of the Company and the beginnings of direct rule from Britain. It promised to respect all existing treaties and obligations and that Indians would be given employment opportunities under the new regime. Explicit reference was made in it to the fact that all of the Queen's subjects in India, regardless of race, religion or caste, were entitled to equal treatment under the law. It was intended to reassure Indians that the post-1858 settlement was one which would take their interests to heart, and that, at least officially, race would not play a part in colonial policy-making. In purely legal terms, it kept faith with the principles of liberal imperialism and appeared to hold out the promise that British rule would benefit Indians and Britons alike. But as is too often the case with noble statements of faith, reality fell far short of theory, and the failure on the part of the British to live up to the wording of the proclamation would later be used by Indian nationalists as proof of the hollowness of imperial principles (Metcalf, 1994; Mehta, 2000). From the very outset, Indians had been sceptical of such claims, and it is worth noting that at the ceremony in Calcutta intended to mark the proclamation of the Government of India Act, an illumination of Queen Victoria caught fire which led to some cheers from the public.

One of the more concrete manifestations of the sentiments contained in the Queen's proclamation came with the promulgation of the India Councils Act of 1861 that was designed to provide an opportunity for Indian voices to be heard by the government (Moore, 1966). It established a council advisory to the Viceroy on which would serve a small number of Indian representatives carefully selected by the British government. The Indians who sat on it were far from representative. They were instead chosen on the basis of their proven loyalty and they came from a tiny stratum of Indian society: princes and high-ranking Indian officials for the most part. Other opportunities for Indian participation in political decision-making came at the municipal level in 1882 when it was decided to make available a limited number of opportunities for 'respectable' Indians to serve alongside British officials. The decision by the British to create such opportunities, while based in part on the principles of the Queen's proclamation, was also determined by the need to expand the tax base beyond agricultural revenues, and to do so they included representatives of Indian commercial and professional interests so as to secure their acquiescence.

Another manifestation of the attempts to create a modern state came with the emphasis the British placed on acquiring more accurate and complete information about India (Cohn, 1996). The British Raj became an empire of documentation, as the post-1858 period witnessed an acceleration of efforts at knowing and classifying the peoples of India. There was a proliferation of district gazetteers, guidebooks dealing with particular regions and castes, and atlases, all of which were intended to make Indian society more legible and comprehensible to the British. Efforts to codify Indian law so as to reduce dependency upon *pandits* and *maulvis* for interpretation are a further illustration of the priority the British placed on creating systematic and stable forms of knowledge to which they could refer.

The best example of this will to know came with the decision to subject all of British India to a census in 1871. Earlier attempts to count and categorize

Indians had largely taken place at the local level, and there had not been a concerted effort to ensure that the data was collected according to common criteria. The census of 1871 was intended to provide just that. This information would prove to be crucial to British rule, for it allowed them to ground their policies on what they deemed to be objective criteria. Revenue assessments and their impact could be more easily assessed, recruiting efforts could be more effectively targeted, and economic policies implemented on the basis of such information. This data, however, was contaminated from the outset by the assumptions which underpinned it. The widely held belief that the fundamental essences of Indian society were those of religion and caste meant that these became the overarching criteria by which Indians were identified. The fluid social relations that had previously existed became ever more static owing to the manner in which caste and religious differences were inscribed onto Indian society. The allegedly scientific nature of the data produced by the census would sharpen divisions within Indian society that would in turn undermine later efforts by Indian nationalists to develop a common agenda and vocabulary.

The Criminal Tribes Act of 1871 illustrates how colonial ethnography came to inform British policy in India (Nigam, 1990). Drawing on the policies and practices developed in the campaigns against *thagi*, this legislation was aimed at dealing with those communities within India that the British wanted to bring under control, particularly tribal and nomadic groups. We have already mentioned the estimated 60,000 Santals who rose up in revolt in 1855. An uprising among the Gonds in 1879 required six infantry regiments to bring them under control. The *banjara*s were another community identified by the British as a possible threat to security; itinerant grain merchants, they had been vital allies in an earlier period when they helped ensure that colonial armies could be supplied in the field. But they had ceased to fill that function by the second half of the nineteenth century and, in common with other nomadic communities, they had come to be viewed with suspicion on account of their living beyond the bounds of settled society. This legislation allowed whole communities to be effectively criminalized by virtue of their birth which then enabled the British to impose draconian controls over them, including forcible resettlement onto reserves where they would be taught skills and trades intended to make them productive members of society.

If the logic which underpinned legislation like the Criminal Tribes Act illustrates the merging of a conservative focus on ensuring security with a liberal faith in the ability to reform Indian society, the deeper ideological clash between these two streams of thought is captured in the personalities and policies of two Viceroys: Lord Lytton and Lord Ripon. Lytton exemplified the romantic conservatism which coursed through British rule; Ripon the reformist agenda that can be tracked back to Dalhousie, Bentinck and Cornwallis. Lytton, as observed through the planning of the 1877 *Darbar*, had nothing but disdain for western-educated Indians. He put his faith in the representatives of what he thought was authentically Indian, namely the Indian princes who he believed could best ensure that the ultimate objective of political stability was met. He was alarmed by the growing clamour for reform that was emanating from the Indian intelligentsia and not only publicly derided them but also sought to muzzle them through legislation. English and vernacular language newspapers had blossomed in the 1870s and in them can be found many pointed criticisms of his policies: the wastefulness of the *darbar*, the political and economic costs of the war he launched against Afghanistan, the government's failure to alleviate the sufferings of millions of Indians hit hard by the famines of 1876–78, and his decision to abolish the tariffs that were intended to protect Indian markets from being swamped with Lancashire textiles. A number of Indian political cartoons appeared in the 1870s in which British officials and their Indian allies were lampooned (Mitter, 1997). Lytton's response was to introduce the Vernacular Press Act of 1878 to curb the freedom of the Indian press. Freedom of the press was a core principle of liberal values and Lytton's attacks were taken as proof of the divergence of British policy from the principles to which it laid claim.

His successor, Lord Ripon, arrived in India with a much more optimistic view that India could be improved in consultation with western-educated and liberal-minded Indians, the very communities which Lytton had so assiduously shunned. While many of those who held out the greatest hopes for sweeping reforms were ultimately disappointed, these years were marked by a number of efforts to try and re-establish liberal principles of rule. The Vernacular Press Act was repealed shortly after his arrival and in 1882 membership on municipal councils was broadened to include a limited number of elected Indians. But the limits of liberalism would be tested once again when his government tried to introduce some legal reforms in what was known as the Ilbert Bill, named after the law member of the Viceroy's council. The firestorm unleashed by the Ilbert Bill became the litmus test of liberal imperialism, and the outcome was instrumental in convincing Indians of the need to mobilize in order for their aspirations to be heard.

In the drafting of the Ilbert Bill, few officials could have been aware of the controversies that would shortly follow, as the legislation was intended to remove a curious, at least in their eyes, anomaly in the administration of criminal justice in India. Indian judges in the *mofussil* were not allowed to sit in judgment over Europeans charged with criminal activities though they had long enjoyed this authority in the Presidency capitals. As a consequence, Europeans charged with criminal offences outside Calcutta, Madras and Bombay had to be brought to those cities for trial, a costly and time-consuming exercise. This requirement was also in contravention of the spirit if not the exact wording of the Queen's proclamation, and so the government set about giving Indian judges in the *mofussil* the same authority that their counterparts enjoyed in the Presidency capitals. The legislation triggered a ferocious debate in the Anglo-Indian press which was soon transferred to Britain where many returned Anglo-Indians also spoke out vehemently against the Act. Their opposition rested upon the fear that Indian judges could not be trusted to administer the law fairly, and that English women in particular would be vulnerable to abuse by Indian judges. Memories of 1857–58 were very much alive, and with them remained the deeply rooted conviction that European women needed to be protected from Indian males (Sinha, 1995) [*Doc. 33*]. The racism which had so deeply infected Anglo-Indian society rose to the surface, its vehemence catching many by surprise, and, notwithstanding the efforts made by some to defend the principles behind the legislation, the government was forced to backtrack. Indian judges would be allowed to sit in judgment on Europeans, but Europeans would have the right to insist that half the jury be made up of Europeans, and this requirement was also extended to courts in the Presidency capitals which had hitherto not been so restricted. This compromise was a bitter disappointment to many Indians who were stunned by the level of hypocrisy which the debates exposed [*Doc. 34*].

ECONOMIES AND COMMUNITIES UNDER STRAIN

Rebuilding the Indian economy after the shockwaves of 1857–58 had receded was another priority for the British. Of particular importance was the need to ensure that the costs of administering India did not fall on British taxpayers, and with that goal in mind policies were introduced to try and ensure that a steady flow of funds back to Britain was sufficient to cover all the costs of colonial rule. The wealth that was siphoned away from India proved crucial to squaring Britain's balance of payments. By the second half of the nineteenth century, Britain was in a deficit position with respect to its trade with the USA and with Europe, yet with India it was in a position of surplus and could use that surplus to cover its deficits elsewhere. Nationalists like Dadabhai Naoroji and Romesh Chandra Dutt would use the home charges as well as Britain's surplus in its balance of payments with India to develop their drain theory; in essence this argued that the monies taken out of India, while benefiting Britain, deprived India of much-needed capital which, had it remained in Indian hands, could have furthered economic development there.

Direct rule not only intensified pressures on India to meet the demands of the home charges, but also rendered the Indian economy more vulnerable to global economic cycles. The increased penetration of India by British commercial interests, when combined with improvements in transportation, notably railways and steamships, meant that the Indian and imperial economies became more entwined. Exports of raw materials such as cotton, jute, tea, coffee, wheat and oil seeds from India continued to grow, as did imports of manufactured goods from Britain, further facilitated when Lord Lytton removed the tariff barriers that had protected Indian producers from the full onslaught of British textiles. Between 1870 and 1913 India went from third to first place as a destination for British exports. Indian exports, on the other hand, were subject to price swings that exposed Indian cultivators and investors to possible ruin and in some cases starvation. The collapse of the prices paid for many exports in the 1870s contributed substantially to the sufferings caused by the famines later in that decade (Davis, 2000).

Historians continue to debate the validity of the drain theory. The deterioration of craft production in India, especially of cotton goods, is used by its proponents to affirm the detrimental effects of colonial rule on the Indian economy. Critics of the drain theory, while willing to acknowledge that economic policies in India were in the first instance guided by the needs of Britain rather than India as proved by the discriminatory tariff system in place, are not so convinced that economic policies were consistently regressive. They point, for example, to the emergence of Indian entrepreneurs in places like Ahmadabad who invested in mills where large-scale production could occur, as well as the many examples of small-scale industries emerging in India (Roy, 2000). More generally, they have argued that the domestic market in India was so large that it could accommodate British imports and Indian output without too much strain. The internal market in India for textiles can be subdivided into three: a luxury market, a middle-class market, and the mass market. British imports are argued to have had little impact on the first of these as such textiles were ill-suited to machine production and they were also very culturally specific. The mass market was also largely protected; it was the middle zone that felt the impact the most. Moreover, colonial rule created new demands for commodities which were met by Indian producers. While such arguments have introduced some caveats to the earlier picture of economic stagnation and impoverishment, sufficient questions remain about the intentions and consequences of colonial economic policies to suggest that, while colonial rule might have created opportunities for some, a great many Indians did not experience any of these benefits.

Raw materials were not the only items that were being exported in ever greater quantities in the decades after the rebellion. So too were the growing numbers of Indians themselves, who became a valuable source of labour for an expanding British Empire. There was a long history of Indians migrating overseas in search of trading opportunities. Tamil-speaking peasants and merchants from South India had crossed over into Sri Lanka, where they would figure prominently as both petty traders and labourers on the tea plantations that began to dot the landscape from the 1840s. But over the course of the nineteenth century, and especially from the 1870s, a combination of push and pull factors led to a tremendous increase in the numbers of Indian migrants who would contribute to Indian diasporas around the globe.

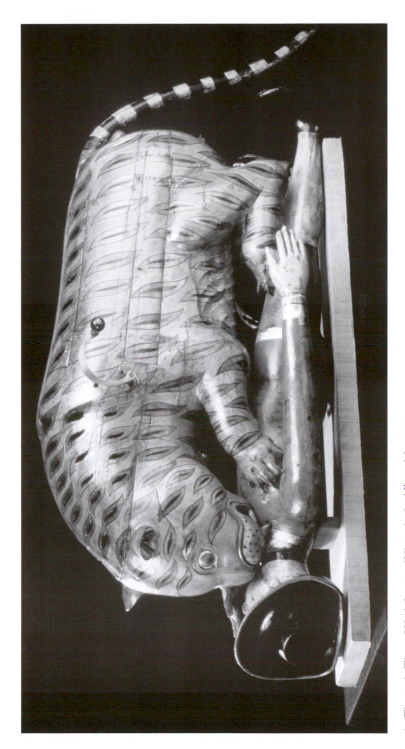

1. Tippoo's Tiger, V&A Images/Victoria & Albert Museum

2. *A View in the Bazaar, leading to the Chitpore Road, Calcutta,* c.1820, aquatint of a painting by James Baillie Fraser, 1826, British Library, X644(24), plate 24

3. *Mahadaji Sindhia entertaining a British Naval Officer and Military Officer with a nautch*, c.1820, British Library, Add. Or. 1: 19553

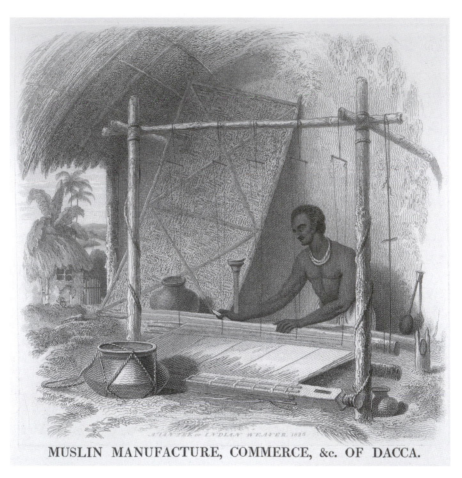

MUSLIN MANUFACTURE, COMMERCE, &c. OF DACCA.

4. *A Tantee or Indian Weaver*, 1827, etching after a painting by Sir Charles D'Oyly, British Library X628(16), plate 16

5. *Procession of a Hindoo Woman to the Funeral Pile of Her Husband*, c.1783, engraving of a painting by William Hodges, British Library W2126(9), plate 9

Thugs stabbing the Eyes and bodies of the
travellers whom they have strangled, preparatory
to throwing them into a Well.

6. *Thugs Mutilating the Bodies*, c.1829–1840, British Library, Add. 41300 c5575-05

JUSTICE.

7. Justice, *Punch*, 12 September 1857

8. The Residency at Lucknow, photograph, Robert and Harriet Tytler, 1858, British Library, Photo 32/(12), 12

9. *Bombay Girls School*, 1867, lithograph of a painting by William Simpson, British Library X108(11), plate 11

Population pressures, land shortages, revenue demands and the erosion of many of India's traditional industries drove many Indians out of their villages in search of employment. While many would migrate to new locations within India, still more would be forced to look overseas. Most of these became caught up in a system of indentured labour, which appropriately has been termed 'A New System of Slavery' (Tinker, 1974). Between 1834 and 1920, just over 1.2 million Indians left India as indentured labourers (Northrup, 1999: 89). The contracts which indentured labourers signed obliged them to serve for terms of from five to ten years working elsewhere in the British Empire, for which they received little pay. The growth of the imperial economy when coupled to the ending of the slave trade in 1807 and subsequent abolition of slavery in 1833 caused a shortage of agricultural labourers in many parts of the British Empire. The British looked to India to fill this vacuum, and tens of thousands of Indians left for the sugar plantations of the West Indies, Mauritius, Natal and Fiji. More would follow to help build railways in Africa and work on the rubber plantations of Malaysia. While indentured labourers were entitled to return passage once they had completed their term abroad, many chose to stay in places like Fiji, South Africa and the Caribbean where they carved out niches for themselves as small merchants and moneylenders.

It was over the course of the 1870s that a number of latent pressures within Indian society began to work their way to the surface. A flourishing public sphere, occasioned by the proliferation of vernacular newspapers, periodicals and inexpensive books as well as street theatre and various voluntary associations, fostered debates within Indian society as to the impact of colonial rule and the social and economic changes with which Indians were faced (Freitag, 1989). The debate over widow remarriage alone triggered the establishment of at least twenty-five vernacular newspapers in Bengal. The explosion of printed material in India was to have profound long-term consequences, for the novels and essays that were produced not only prompted discussions about the condition of India but also helped initiate debates about differences within India. Language played a crucial role as technological advances allowed most vernaculars to take on a printed form. Throughout much of northern India, the vernacular spoken language was Hindustani. However, when written in the Sanskrit Devanagari script, it became Hindi and when written in Persian script, it became Urdu. Tamil, Bengali, Marathi and a host of other vernaculars were also employed as a means of expressing their communities' cultural aspirations, all of which helped to encourage a growing sense of uniqueness within each of the many regions in India.

The increasing alienation of the Indian elite from colonial rule, which Mahatma Gandhi would declare in 1909 in *Hind Swaraj* to be the desire to have 'English rule without the English', became more visible. The *bhadralok* found that their authority and influence were being challenged from a number of directions. Colonial officials were increasingly critical of the *babu*s, and, despite an official rhetoric of toleration and incorporation, made it difficult for them to secure well-paying positions within the government. At the same time, the leadership aspirations of the *bhadralok* were undermined by peasant assertiveness as well as a growing sense of distinctiveness amongst the Muslim population.

Colonial policy played an important role in the sharpening of religious and caste divisions within Indian society. The censuses conducted after 1871 required that people in India be placed within clear-cut religious categories, and when Indians failed to identify their religious identities, enumerators were expected to list them as either Hindu or Muslim. Fixing people into such watertight compartments not only made permanent what had in the past been much more fluid, but it also accentuated religious and caste divisions in such a way as to foster rivalries and resentments, especially when religious and caste identities coincided with economic or political differences or provided material or cultural entitlements (Pandey, 1990). Social and economic tensions were therefore easily recast in religious terms. One of the more concrete expressions of this intensified appeal to religious identities in northern India came with the emergence of Cow Protection Leagues. Cows acquired a particularly poignant symbolism in an era when social and cultural identities were in flux, and by rallying to the cow bridges could be formed between high-caste and low-caste Hindus as they pitted themselves against alien intruders, be they British or Muslim. Southern India also witnessed similar situations in which religion masked a complex interplay of economic and social grievances. The Mappilas, Muslim cultivators who lived on the Malabar Coast in present-day Kerala, found themselves under British rule following annexation in 1799. The region had previously been part of the empire of Haidar Ali and Tipu Sultan. Following the British conquest, high-caste landlords were reintroduced into the area, a number of whom had been expelled by Tipu Sultan. Muslim tenants lost much of their autonomy and their resentment took on religious overtones, bursting into revolt on many occasions in the nineteenth and twentieth centuries (Panikkar, 1988).

Many of the debates within this public sphere focused on issues of social reform. By appealing to a sense of community, framed in terms of Hindu values and culture, community leaders were able to counter the British while re-establishing authority over those elements of society who threatened the existing social order, notably low-caste groups and women. In *Anandamath* (the Abbey of Bliss), published in 1882, Bankimcandra Chatterji used the Sanyasi Rebellion in the 1770s, wherein the villain was the Mughal governor, to incite Bengalis to unite against the occupiers. Bankimcandra was born into an orthodox Brahmin household and, while he was educated at Calcutta University and served as a deputy magistrate under the British, his written works reveal a sense of the Indian nation as being defined in terms of a revived and rationalized form of Hinduism. The Mughals here were intended to serve as metaphors for the British. Yet the juxtaposition of oppressed Hindu peasants against rapacious Muslim landlords helped to nurture the impression that Bengal was Hindu, and that the Muslims were, like the British, alien intruders. The song 'Bande Mataram', or 'Hail to the Mother', was taken from *Anandamath* and became a rallying cry for Indian nationalists, and continues to be popular amongst Hindu nationalists in India today.

One of the most powerful and influential expressions of Hindu nationalism came with the foundation by Dayananda Saraswati of the Arya Samaj in Bombay in 1875. The popularity of this socio-religious reform movement would, however, be greater to the north, in the Punjab and the areas around Delhi, as it was in that region that religious competition between Hindus, Muslims and Sikhs was most intense. Like Rammohun Roy, Dayananda Saraswati was outraged by what he deemed to be the deterioration of Hindu religious and ethical beliefs, and the subsequent degradation of society including the practice of untouchability, idolatry and child marriage (Jones, 1989). He also deliberately chose to use vernacular languages rather than Sanskrit as a means of reaching out to the masses. Yet he differed from Roy in his strident defence of Indian society from what he saw as the pernicious influences of Christianity as well as in his commitment to win back converts to Islam and Christianity. While Saraswati, like other religious nationalists, was critical of western Christianity and its preoccupation with material rather than spiritual progress, he did not completely reject the West. Modern communications technology, including the mass media, as well as railways, was put to use. A major problem that he faced, however, was that unlike the other major world religions, Hindu thought had never really engaged with the question of conversion for one was born a Hindu, one did not become a Hindu. But in order to win back Indians who had been attracted to other religions, which was particularly acute in the Punjab where Islam and Sikhism had long attracted converts and where Christian missions were becoming very active, Saraswati developed rituals so as to welcome one-time Hindus back into the fold.

Muslim society in India also became more actively engaged in the 1870s in articulating a sense of identity and trying to chart a course forward. But just as was the case with other Indian communities, there were differences of opinion as to how to achieve their goals. Moreover, Muslims in India had to contend with not only the extent to which their authority and status had diminished since the time of the Mughals but also with the suspicion entertained by many British officials that they were the chief instigators of the Indian Rebellion. Muslims in India responded to these challenges in a variety of ways. Muhammad Abid Husayn, through the school or madrasa he established in Deoband in 1868, sought to regenerate Islam in India through classical Islamic education, particularly the close scrutiny of the Koran and Islamic legal commentaries (Metcalf, 1982).

An alternative approach was pursued by Syed Ahmed Khan who set up the Muhammadan Anglo-Oriental College at Aligarh in 1875 for the purpose of introducing western science and scholarship into Muslim intellectual life (Lelyveld, 1996). Education, he believed, would help to heal the breach between the British and their Muslim subjects. In 1858 he had argued in *The Causes of the Indian Revolt* that the rebellion was the product of a breakdown in relations between ruler and ruled. Syed Ahmed Khan also undertook other measures to ease tensions between Indian Muslims and the British. He wrote a number of essays and pamphlets designed to counter the Islamophobic writings in circulation after 1857 by portraying Islam in a more favourable light. In late 1870 he launched a new periodical, the *Mohammedan Social Reformer*, in which he could promulgate plans to reform Muslim society. Yet Syed Ahmed Khan was no radical; while extolling the values of western education, he did not wish to see it extended to Muslim women. Nor did he come out strongly against the practice of *purdah*, or the seclusion of women. While the rationalist approach adopted by Syed Ahmed Khan proved to be more appealing to the British, in the long run the traditionalist Deoband School, which was feared by the British because of its similarities to Wahabism, had greater impact on Muslims in India and what would become Pakistan.

A common feature throughout these intensified debates among Indians about how best to reconcile tradition with the changes happening about them was the central role accorded to questions of gender (Sarkar, 2001). Great symbolic weight was attached to women throughout this period. For the British, as we have already seen, the condition of women question had become one of the yardsticks by which they measured the state of civilization amongst their subjects. *Sati*, child marriage, *purdah* and widow remarriage were all issues around which commentators mobilized support for reform. And for British women, saving their Indian sisters from what they believed to be the cruel conditions in which they were kept confined was instrumental in helping them define for themselves a role within imperialism (Burton, 1994). By participating as nurses, missionaries and educators, British women could penetrate deeply into domestic society and, so it was hoped, begin to effect the changes needed. For observers like Rudyard Kipling, their efforts were an important contribution to Britain's civilizing mission [*Doc. 35*]. The opening up of schools and hospitals for women was celebrated as examples of the benefits which British rule brought to Indian women [see plate 9].

Indian commentators were equally preoccupied with the issue of gender for, like the British, identifying the roles expected of women within society at large became part of the means by which they could achieve a properly and morally ordered society. Indian commentators in particular objected to the ways in which colonial officials not only sought to impose their values on Indian society, but also purported to speak on behalf of Indian women.

The growing independence of middle-class women, for example, witnessed in their growing presence within the public sphere, threatened patriarchal society in one of the few areas where Indian males felt they still possessed some authority: the home. Bengali cartoons of the 1870s mocked Indian males who were depicted as having been emasculated by the twin forces of colonial rule and domineering and independent-minded women (Mitter, 1997). Consequently, traditions were asserted or in some cases reworked in such a way as to bolster the authority of those groups which had suffered loss of status and authority under colonial rule. Respectability became ever more important in this context, which meant that women were not only expected to fulfil their domestic duties but they also increasingly became charged with maintaining religious rites and traditions which were under attack.

While many of these debates over the place of women in Indian society echoed what had been heard earlier over the issue of *sati*, a new twist emerged as women's voices came to be heard. A number of Indian women made important and original contributions to the question of reform, for while they identified in broad terms with the need for Indian society to be reformed, they did not simply subscribe to the views being foisted upon them by colonial reformers. Nor did they necessarily concede to the points made by male Indian reformers. Instead, they advocated reforms but from within their own understanding of what tradition and custom ought to mean. Tarabai Shinde, a member of a well-off Maratha family, wrote *A Comparison between Women and Men* in 1882 as a response to the public outcry that followed the sensational trial and the subsequent sentencing (initially to be hanged but remitted to transportation) of a young Brahmin widow for infanticide. The young widow, Vijaylakshmi, who was only 24, admitted that a dead baby that had been found was hers, and that she had killed it to avoid the shame that would fall on her and her family were it to become known that she had not lived the chaste life expected of widows, particularly high-caste ones like herself. Shinde was outraged by what she saw as yet further proof of the tendency within Indian society to hold women responsible for what had befallen it [*Doc. 36*]. She attacked the hypocrisy of Indian men adopting western ways, aping Englishmen, yet insisting that Indian women conform to a warped sense of Indian traditions. Her criticisms were not directed so much at Hindu customs and practices, but more at the way in which they had not been properly upheld, and for that she held men responsible. Another well-known champion of reform was Pandita Saraswati Ramabai who, following the death of her husband when she was still quite young, had gone to England where she had trained in medicine and converted to Christianity. She became a popular speaker, both in Britain and the USA, and used those opportunities to rally support from women in those countries to assist in improving the lives of women in India. She framed her appeals in domestic terms, arguing that as long as Indian women were denied education, they were ill-suited to the tasks of raising a new generation of Indians who could contribute to the economic, political and social modernization of India [*Doc. 37*].

THE INDIAN NATIONAL CONGRESS AND THE LIMITS OF NATIONALISM

Traditional accounts of the rise of Indian nationalism have fastened onto the first meeting of the Indian National Congress in 1885 as a watershed moment. While later historians have disputed this, pointing out the limited objectives pursued by Congress and the fact that it represented only a thin slice of Indian society, it would over the course of the next sixty years become one of the principal vehicles through which nationalist aspirations could be voiced and support mobilized. Moreover, in its blend of political moderation and attempts to be as inclusive as possible, it became a model for other nationalist movements elsewhere in the colonial world, including the African National Congress in South Africa. While all this has become apparent through the benefits of hindsight, at the time the potential of the Indian National Congress would have appeared much more limited. Just over seventy educated Indians met in Bombay to share their experiences and opinions on life under colonial rule and to consider ways of working together.

While this was the first India-wide attempt at fashioning a collective response to colonial rule, it had been preceded by a number of regional and local organizations committed to various political and social reform agendas. In Bengal, for example, Surendranath Banerjea (1848–1925), who would play a critical role in the subsequent history of the Indian National Congress, had been instrumental in founding the Indian Association in Calcutta in 1876. Bombay, Pune, Lahore, Allahabad and Madras were home to similar organizations where middle-class and English-educated Indians for the most part came together to try and lobby the British government for changes to colonial policy. Foremost amongst their demands were tax relief, reductions in military spending, increased opportunities for Indians within the civil service, and more prospects for Indians to sit on government councils and committees. The decision to move towards an India-wide campaign was largely due to the lessons they had learned from the Ilbert Bill agitation – not only had that experience exposed the deep racial rift between them and their rulers but they were also shown how effective lobbying could be if it could count upon the mobilization of the wider community, as they had witnessed happening among the British expatriate community in India.

A number of the representatives who came to Bombay in 1885 also brought with them grievances against the ways in which the British had deliberately sought to exclude them from positions of employment in the Indian Civil Service. Despite the explicit promise in the Queen's proclamation that race would not be a barrier, many found their expectations dashed as the British used a number of stratagems to try and frustrate Indian ambitions. For a period of time, applicants were required to sit an exam which was only administered in Britain, age restrictions were rigorously enforced to try and prevent Indians who had taken extra training so as to master the syllabus expected of candidates for the civil service, and a number of other obstacles were thrown up. Surendranath Banerjea had actually overcome most of these but eventually was thrown out on trumped-up charges that he had lied about his date of birth when in fact he had calculated it according to Indian custom rather than British practice. Clearly, while British India was officially colour blind, race did matter in daily administration, even at the highest levels, and these contradictions fed into the *bhadralok*'s growing sense of disenchantment. Romesh Chandra Dutt exemplified this early generation of nationalists. A western-educated Bengali, who rose as high as Indians could within the Indian Civil Service, he applied his knowledge and interest in economics and political science to the study of India's problems and published a number of histories as well as economic and political studies. Dadabhai Naoroji, who presided over the second annual meeting of the Indian National Congress in 1886 (and would return as president in 1893 and 1906), was from Bombay, and like Dutt he employed his training in law, politics and economics to examine India's problems. Together, Dutt and Naoroji focused on the negative consequences of colonial rule, popularizing the notion of a drain on India's economy. They were not romantic nationalists, hearkening back to some kind of idealized past. Instead, they both subscribed to the view that western forms of political and social organization were often superior, and that the western emphasis on individual rights and responsibilities would have a liberating effect on Indian society. The problem they identified, however, was that the British did not live up to their high ideals. Naoroji would later take his criticisms to London where, having been elected as a Liberal MP to Parliament for the London constituency of Central Finsbury, he used his term in office (1892–95) to highlight India's plight before Parliament.

Not surprisingly, given the kinds of grievances that lay behind the first Congress, ones for the most part grounded in issues of employment opportunities and political participation, we find that most of the delegates were western-educated lawyers and officials, mainly Hindu and often from Bengal or Bombay. Their language was moderate in tone, and they used a political vocabulary with which the British were familiar. The bigger and to some more intractable questions of social reform, of addressing the crushing poverty seen throughout India, and even of self-determination were rarely broached in the early meetings. Instead, representatives at these meetings were careful to pledge their loyalty to British rule, and rather than seek to overthrow the British, they chose instead to press for limited amelioration [*Doc. 38*]. Noticeably absent were leaders from the Muslim community. Figures like Syed Ahmed Khan, while sharing some of the broad objectives that were under discussion, felt that Congress did not nor could it represent

India's Muslims. Already, there was a sense within some intellectuals in India that one's identity was grounded in one's religious faith, thereby establishing some of the preconditions for the two-nation argument that would result in the catastrophic partitioning of India in 1947. There were no Indian princes at the meeting, nor any rural voices to be heard. It was instead a meeting of like-minded western-educated urban intellectuals, a tiny yet influential segment of Indian society. The subsequent history of the Indian National Congress would be marked by a series of efforts, some more successful than others, to try and broaden its support. For their part, British officials would employ a number of strategies intended to prevent a coalescing of opposition to colonial rule. Yet neither Congress nor the British could ever fully master, much less control, the diverse demands and pressures within Indian society.

CHAPTER FIVE

THE LEGACIES OF EMPIRE IN BRITAIN AND INDIA

Anyone visiting Britain or India will find telling signs of the long and complex history of interaction between the two. It is estimated that restaurant-goers in Britain spend nearly £2 billion annually in Indian restaurants, and that the amount of mango chutney sold in the United Kingdom tops £7 million. That it has come to this was interestingly foretold nearly two centuries ago when a contributor to the *Oriental Herald*, a magazine established in Britain for returned Anglo-Indians, wrote in September 1828, 'from the excellence of the dishes that the Indian condiments are capable of producing, coupled with the cheapness with which rice is now to be had in this country, we think it probably that at no distant period curry and rice will become one of the national dishes of England'. Chip shops in Glasgow offering haggis pakoras, the cross-over success of *bhangra* music, and periodic bouts of imperial nostalgia as evidenced in the popularity of many Merchant and Ivory films attest to the grip that India continues to have on British culture. Yet the recent outbreaks of racial violence in northern British cities and the growing alienation of Asian youth suggests that there remains in Britain a strong undercurrent of the racism that became such a pervasive characteristic of imperial rule. There is, however, a danger in exaggerating India's imprint on the lives of people back in Britain. Comparatively few served in India, slightly more might know someone who had been to India, Indian affairs only fitfully engaged Parliament, and, while the British consumed large amounts of Indian tea, it is difficult to sustain the claim that they necessarily connected what they were drinking back to the empire (though by the end of the nineteenth century advertisers were trying to get them to do that). At its peak, the number of Britons domiciled in India reached just over 185,000 (1911). Most of these were congregated in the larger centres where they could live lives that were insulated from their Indian surroundings.

Half a globe away English continues to be the favoured language of India's intellectual and business elite, the country's most prestigious schools and colleges would not be out of place in Britain, the vitality of the Indian press and the international success enjoyed by Indian authors writing in

English are testimonials to the lingering effects of Britain on India. So too, according to some, is India's relatively favourable experience of democracy in the years since independence in 1947. But again imperialism left its scars on Indian society. Economic development was impeded by colonial rule; when the British departed in 1947, India was still largely an agrarian society, much the same as it had been when the British began to break out of their coastal enclaves in the mid-eighteenth century. India was still subject to famine: some 3 million died in Bengal and Bihar as recently as 1942–43. Education, while benefiting India's elite, had not trickled that deeply into Indian society. The partition and the ongoing struggles over Kashmir are a legacy of the growing separation of Hindus and Muslims which colonial rule fostered. So too is the brutal civil war that has plagued Sri Lanka for the past two decades, for many of the Tamil separatists were migrants brought to Sri Lanka to work on British-owned tea plantations.

To explain and account for this very mixed bag of legacies both in Britain and India, we need only to remind ourselves of the several paradoxes noted at the outset which were such important defining characteristics of colonial India. The British came to India not to establish a settler colony as they did in the Americas or Australia but to trade. Profits were their objective, and the priority assigned to ensuring a steady return on trade with India influenced subsequent policies. At the same time, commercial objectives could not always be easily reconciled with growing territorial ambitions and the imperatives of colonial rule. Moreover, the British only slowly acquired the knowledge and means to impose their authority and so were not only dependent from the very outset on trying to work within Indian structures and cultural practices, but also relied upon Indians for commercial expertise, capital and military labour. While these dependencies would weaken over time, and be accompanied by a growing tendency to disparage Indian customs and traditions, as events in 1857 only too graphically demonstrated, the British could only disregard India at great risk. And so the oft-quoted commitment to liberal principles of economic progress, social reform and individual liberty were all too often sacrificed to concerns over security as well as to the growing conviction that no matter how desirable such principles might be in theory, India was just not ready for them. This discounting of India's potential was anchored in the belief in India's inherent difference from the West, a point of view that was sustained by the manner in which knowledge of India was collected, analysed and disseminated.

PART FOUR   DOCUMENTS

DOCUMENT 1   JAMES FITZJAMES STEPHEN, 'KAYE'S HISTORY OF
             THE INDIAN MUTINY', 1864

Kaye was one of the most prolific writers on nineteenth century India and his history of the Indian Mutiny is one of the standard works on the mutiny. In this review, James Fitzjames Stephen captures not only the pride and wonderment with which the British viewed their conquest of India, but also demonstrates the many ways by which the British drew stark differentiations between themselves and Indians, and between the various communities in India.

Perhaps we may safely say that on the whole it forms one of the most extraordinary stories that modern history contains. It is difficult to imagine anything more striking to the imagination than our Indian Empire, with the marvellous contrast which it presents between the rulers and the subjects. On the one side there is a vast country peopled and cultivated in most parts for thousands of years, but interspersed with immense wastes, virgin forests, and mighty mountain ranges, the haunts of wild beasts and of men equally wild. All over this immense region are scattered the ruins of successive dynasties of conquerors. At Delhi, a few years ago, there still lived the representative of the Great Mogul. . . . The whole land was a sort of wilderness of creeds and races. Mahometans, Hindoos, Buddhists, Parsees, Sikhs, Afghans, Ghoorkas, wild aboriginal tribes, little less savage than the beasts of the forests; strange sects with their own wild laws and customs, all lived together in a kind of organized confusion, under institutions of which some were as old as the dawn of authentic history, whilst others, and very great ones, were things, so to speak, of yesterday, the fruit of armed invasion by fierce mountaineers. They had, however, one common quality. Neither Mahometan nor Hindoo, Sikh or Mahratta, had in him any power of improvement or any wish for it. . . . Amongst all these heterogeneous millions were scattered in mere driblets a few thousand white men and women, who in some respects might fairly be called picked specimens of the very soul and spirit of Europe. They were amongst the sturdiest members of the sturdiest race in the world. In courage, spirit, and personal strength, they were more than a match for the most warlike Mahratta or Afghan. Their countrymen had constantly fought and frequently conquered, both by sea and land, the greatest and bravest nations of Europe, and had peopled with their blood, and governed by their institutions, the best part of the habitable world, They themselves were almost universally gentlemen – men of education and generous sentiment. Of late years they had also been almost universally religious men – religious no doubt, in a rather narrow way, but intensely in earnest about it. Probably no body of men in the world ever held more firmly the great Protestant doctrine which is characteristically inscribed on the Royal Exchange – 'The earth is the Lord's and the fullness thereof, the round world, and that they dwell therein'.

Religion, as they viewed it, had little to do with art, with tenderness, with consolation under the inevitable evils of life, with raptures or contemplation, but it had everything to do with life and government.

Fraser's Magazine 70 (1864): 765–6

DOCUMENT 2   J.R. SEELEY, *THE EXPANSION OF ENGLAND*, 1971

Seeley's History *has long been viewed as a seminal text in imperial historiography. This short extract brings out Seeley's consciousness of the paradoxical nature of colonial rule.*

How can the same nation pursue two lines of policy so radically different without bewilderment, be despotic in Asia and democratic in Australia, be in the East at once the greatest Mussulman Power in the world . . . and at the same time in the West be the foremost champion of free thought and spiritual religions, stand out as a great military Imperialism to resist the march of Russia in Central Asia at the same that it fills Queensland and Manitoba with free settlers.

Classics of British Historical Literature. Chicago: University of Chicago Press, 1971, 141

DOCUMENT 3   ROMESH CHANDRA DUTT (ROMESH CHUNDER
DUTT) *THE ECONOMIC HISTORY OF INDIA UNDER
EARLY BRITISH RULE*, 1906

In his economic history of colonial rule in India, Dutt set out what would become one of the key concepts in modern Indian nationalism, namely that colonial rule acted as a drain on the Indian economy, subordinating Indian needs and frustrating Indian economic development in the interests of the British economy. Yet Dutt, like many of his counterparts, subscribed to the principles of liberal capitalism and hence it was not so much capitalism that he queried, but rather its incomplete and inconsistent application by the British.

It is, unfortunately, a fact which no well-informed Indian official will ignore, that, in many ways, the sources of national wealth in India have been narrowed under British rule. India in the eighteenth century was a great manufacturing as well as a great agricultural country, and the products of the Indian loom supplied the markets of Asia and of Europe. It is, unfortunately, true that the East India Company and the British Parliament, following the selfish commercial policy of a hundred years ago, discouraged India manufacturers in the early years of British rule in order to encourage the rising manufacturers of England. Their fixed policy, pursued during the last decades of the eighteenth century and the first decades of the nineteenth, was to make

India subservient to the industries of Great Britain, and to make the Indian people grow raw produce only, in order to supply material for the looms and manufactories of Great Britain. This policy was pursued with unwavering resolution and with fatal success; orders were sent out, to force Indian artisans to work in the Company's factories; commercial residents were legally vested with extensive powers over villages and communities of Indian weavers; prohibitive tariffs excluded Indian silk and cotton goods from England; English goods were admitted into India free of duty or on payment of a nominal duty. . . . They considered India as a vast estate or plantation, the profits of which were to be withdrawn from India and deposited in Europe.

From the Rise of the British Power in 1757 to the Accession of Queen Victoria in 1837,
2nd edn. London: K. Paul, Trench, Trübner, 1906, ix–x, xiv

DOCUMENT 4	**FIRISHTAH AND DOW, *THE HISTORY OF HINDOSTAN,* 1770**

In his annotated translation of Firishtah's History, *Dow presents his readers with what would become the dominant image of eighteenth century India, namely that it was wracked by political discord and saddled with misgovernment. Such impressions would provide an important rationale for British rule in India.*

The advantages of a conquest of Hindostan to this country are obvious. It would pay as much of the national debt, as government should please to discharge. Should the influx of wealth raise the price of the necessaries and conveniences of life, the poor, on the other hand, by being eased of most of their taxes, would be more able to purchase them. But, say some grave moralists, how can such a scheme be reconciled to justice and humanity? This is an objection of no weight. Hindostan is, at present, torn to pieces by factions. All laws, divine and human, are trampled under foot. Instead of one tyrant, as in the times of the empire, the country now groans under thousands; and the voice of the oppressed multitude reaches heaven. It would, therefore, be promoting the cause of justice and humanity, to pull those petty tyrants from the height to which their villainies have raised them, and to give to so many millions of mankind, a government founded upon the principles of virtue and justice. This task is no less glorious than it is practicable; for it might be accomplished with half the blood which is often expended in Europe, upon an ideal system of a balance of power, and in commercial wars, which must be attended with little éclat, as they are destitute of striking and beneficial consequences.

2nd edn. London: Printed for T. Becket and P.A. de Hondt, 1770, II, 239–40

DOCUMENT 5   WILLIAM WILSON HUNTER, *ANNALS OF RURAL BENGAL*, 1897

Hunter, a British official in India, wrote one of the earliest detailed ethnohistories of rural society in India during a period of profound change. Hunter was struck by the lack of local historical awareness which he contrasts with the sense of history to be found in contemporary Britain. The absence of a historical consciousness (at least as defined according to British terms) provides proof not only of the difference between the British and their Indian subjects but also confirms British superiority for a 'proper' appreciation of the past is necessary to foster a sense of community and encourage a commitment to progress.

It is a matter of regret that an ethnical frontier which must have seen and suffered so much that would be interesting to mankind to know, should be without any record of the past. Every county, almost every parish, in England, has its annals; but in India, vast provinces, greater in extent than the British Islands, have no individual history whatever. Districts that have furnished the sites of famous battles, or lain upon the routes of imperial progresses, appear, indeed, for a moment in the general records of the country; but before the eye has become familiar with their uncouth names, the narrative passes on, and they are forgotten. Nor are the inhabitants themselves very much better acquainted with the history of the country in which they live. Each field, indeed, has its annals. The crops which it has borne during the past century, the rent which it has paid, the occasions on which it has changed hands, the old standing disputes about its watercourses and landmarks, all these are treasured up with sufficient precision. But the bygone joys and sorrows of the district in general, its memorable vicissitudes, its remarkable men, the decline of the old forms of industry and the rise of the new – in a word, all the weightier matters of rural history, are forgotten. . . . Each house scrupulously preserves its own archives, but carefully conceals them from its neighbours.

7th edn. London: Smith, Elder & Co., 1897, 3–4

DOCUMENT 6   RUDYARD KIPLING, 'CHOLERA CAMP', 1896

Death and disease were recurring themes in the public and private writings of the British in India, and no disease was so closely associated with India as was cholera which struck quickly and without warning, leading to many deaths. In describing an outbreak of cholera in a British regiment (British soldiers were not only the most numerous Europeans in India but they were often the most exposed to disease), Kipling not only vividly recreates the traumatic effects of cholera, but demonstrates his keen ear for the idioms and accents of the soldiers of the time.

We've got the cholerer in camp – it's worse than forty fights;
We're dyin' in the wilderness the same as Isrulites;
It's before us, an' be'ind us, an' we cannot get away,
An' the doctor's just reported we've ten more to-day!

Oh, strike your camp an' go, the bugle's callin',
   The Rains are fallin' –
The dead are bushed an' stoned to keep 'em safe below.
The Band's a-doin' all she knows to cheer us;
The Chaplain's gone and prayed to Gawd to 'ear us –
   To 'ear us –
O Lord, for it's a-killin' of us so!

Since August, when it started, it's been stickin' to our tail,
Though they've 'ad us out by marches an' they've 'ad us back by rail;
But it runs as fast as troop-trains, and we cannot get away;
An' the sick-list to the Colonel makes ten more to-day.

There ain't no fun in women nor there ain't no bite to drink;
It's much too wet for shootin', we can only march and think;
An' at evenin', down the nullahs, we can 'ear the jackals say,
"Get up, you rotten beggars, you've ten more to-day!"

'Twould make a monkey cough to see our way o' doin' things –
Lieutenants takin' companies an' captains takin' wings,
An' Lances actin' Sergeants – eight file to obey –
For we've lots o' quick promotion on ten deaths a day!

Our Colonel's white an' twitterly – 'e gets no sleep nor food,
But mucks about in 'orspital where nothing does no good.
'E sends us 'eaps o' comforts, all bought from 'is pay –
But there aren't much comfort 'andy on ten deaths a day.

Our Chaplain's got a banjo, an' a skinny mule 'e rides,
An' the stuff 'e says an' sings us, Lord, it makes us split our sides!
With 'is black coat-tails a-bobbin' to "Ta-ra-ra Boom-der-ay!"
'E's the proper kind o' padre for ten deaths a day.

An' Father Victor 'elps 'im with our Roman Catholicks –
He knows an 'eap of Irish songs an' rummy conjurin'-tricks;
An' the two they works together when it comes to play or pray;
So we keep the ball a-rollin' on ten deaths a day.

We've got the cholerer in camp – we've got it 'ot an' sweet;
It ain't no Christmas dinner, but it's 'elped an' we must eat.
We've gone beyond the funkin', 'cause we've found it doesn't pay,
An' we're rockin' round the Districk on ten deaths a day!

Then strike your camp an' go, the Rains are fallin',
    The bugle's callin'!
The dead are bushed an' stoned to keep 'em safe below!
An' them that do not like it they can lump it,
An' them that cannot stand it they can jump it;
We've got to die somewhere – some way – some'ow –
We might as well begin to do it now!
Then, Number One, let down the tent-pole slow,
Knock out the pegs an' 'old the corners – so!
Fold in the flies, furl up the ropes, an' stow!
Oh, strike – oh, strike your camp an' go!
    (Gawd 'elp us!)

First appeared in *Barrack Room Ballads*, second series, 1896, reprinted
in Rudyard Kipling, *Verses 1889–1896*. vol. 11, *The Writings in Prose and
Verse of Rudyard Kipling*. London: Macmillan, 1898

DOCUMENT 7 ROBERT CLIVE TO COURT OF DIRECTORS, 1765

*Robert Clive's letter to the Court of Directors provides one of the earliest
explicit indications of an imperial ambition emerging within the East India
Company. The status quo was no longer tenable: the British would have to
subdue all their potential rivals otherwise they would lose what they had
acquired so far.*

We have at last arrived at that critical period, which I have long foreseen;
I mean the period which renders it necessary for us to determine whether we
can, or shall, take the whole to ourselves. Sujah Dowla is beat from his
dominion; we are in possession of it, and it is scarcely hyperbole to say,
tomorrow the whole Mogul Empire will be in our power: a large army of
Europeans will effectually preserve us sovereigns. You will, I am sure,
imagine with me, that after the length we have run, the princes of Hindostan
must conclude our views to be boundless; they have seen such instances of
our ambition, that they cannot suppose us capable of moderation; the very
Nabobs whom we might support would be either covetous of our possessions
or jealous of our power. Ambition, fear, avarice, would be daily watching to
destroy us; a victory would be but a temporary relief to us, for the dethron-
ing of the first Nabob would be followed by setting up another. We must,
indeed, become Nabobs ourselves, in fact, if not in name; perhaps so totally

without disguise; but on this subject I cannot be certain until my arrival in Bengal. Let us, without delay, complete our three European regiments to 1000 each; these, with 500 light cavalry, three or four regiments of artillery, and the forces of the country, will certainly render us invincible: in short, if riches and security are the objects of the Company, this is the method, the only method now, for securing them.

> April 1765, in *British India Analyzed: The Provincial and Revenue Establishments of Tippoo Sultaun and of Mahomedan and British Conquerors in Hindostan, Stated and Considered in Three Parts*. London: E. Jeffery, 1793, 767–9

DOCUMENT 8   GHULAM HUSAIN KHAN, *THE SEIR MUTAQHERIN; OR VIEW OF MODERN TIMES*, 1789

The Seir Mutaqherin *offers a unique perspective on the turbulence of mid-eighteenth century Bengal for it was written by a well-placed Muslim noble-man who was in a position to offer an alternative history to that which was being composed by the British. In this extract, he not only challenges the prevailing myth about the Black Hole of Calcutta but he also points to the double standards which prevail in British narratives.*

The truth is, that the Hindustanees wanting only to secure them for the night, as they were to be presented the next morning to the Prince, shut them up in what they heard was a prison in the fort, without having any idea of the capacity of the room; and indeed the English themselves had none of it. This much is certain, that this event, which cuts so capital a figure in Mr. Watt's performance, is not known in Bengal, and even in Calcutta it is ignored by every man out of the four hundred thousand that inhabit that city. . . . Were we therefore to accuse the Indians of cruelty, for such a thoughtless action, we would of course accuse the English, who intending to embark four hundred Gentoo sipahees [Hindu sepoys], destined for Madras, put them in boats, without one single necessary, and at last left them to be overset by the bore, where they all perished, after a three days sail.

> *Being a History of India from the Year 1118 to the Year 1194 of the Hedjrah. Containing in General, the Reign of the Seven Last Emperors of Hindostan, and, in Particular, an Account of the Wars in Bengal.* Calcutta: NP, 1789

DOCUMENT 9   ROBERT ORME, 'HISTORY OF THE PROVINCE OF BENGAL', (C.1762)

Robert Orme, whose histories of the period combined personal observations with extensive examination of the many documents which he collected (and which later led to him being made the official historian of the East India

Company), recounts here the prescience of Alivardi Khan who predicted later British reactions. Alivardi Khan, Nawab of Bengal (1740–1756), declared that his grandson, Siraj-ad-Daula, would succeed him. Mir Jafar, who led the conspiracy against Siraj-ad-Daula, married Alivardi Khan's half-sister.

Mr Scrafton . . . was informed by persons of rank at the court, that the Nabob Allaverdy, on hearing of the murder of Nazir Jang, on the coast of Coromandel, in 1750, said more than once, that the Europeans would conquer the whole country, and he advised his successor to keep a watchful eye over them; but Meer Jaffer affirmed to Mr Scrafton that Allaverdy used to compare the Europeans to a hive of bees, who furnished honey whilst left in peace, but who, if disturbed, would sting their aggressors, and defend themselves to death.

MSS Eur C21, p. 78, Oriental and India Office Collections, British Library, c.1762

DOCUMENT 10   **MIRZA ABU TALEB KHAN, *TRAVELS OF MIRZA ABU TALEB KHAN IN ASIA, AFRICA, AND EUROPE,* 1814**

In this, one of the earliest travelogues written by an Indian traveller to Britain, we can see how Indians, like Europeans, looked at women's roles and used these as a way of assessing other societies. The patriarchal values of the author, a well-educated and well-born Muslim from North India, are apparent and mirror in interesting ways the comments made by European travellers to India.

The English legislators and philosophers have wisely determined, that the best mode of keeping women out of the way of temptation, and their minds from wandering after improper desires, is by giving them sufficient employment; therefore, whatever business can be effected without any great exertion of mental abilities or corporeal strength, is assigned to the women. Thus they have all the internal management and care of the house, and washing the clothes. They are also employed to take care of shops, and, by their beauty and eloquence, often attract customers. This I can speak from my own experience; for I scarcely ever passed the pastry-cook's shop at the corner of Newmanstreet in Oxford-road, that I did not go in and spend some money for the pleasure of talking to a beautiful young woman who kept it. To the men is assigned the business of waiting at table, taking care of the horses and cattle, and management of the garden, farm, etc. This division of labour is attended with much convenience and prevents confusion.

Besides the above important regulation, the English lawgivers have placed the women under many salutary restraints, which prevent their making an improper use of the liberty they have, of mixing in company, and conversing with men. In the first place, strangers, or persons whose characters are not well known, are seldom introduced to them; secondly, the women never visit any bachelor, except he be a near relation; thirdly, no woman of respectability every walks out (in London), unless attended by her husband, a relation, or a confidential servant. They are upon no account allowed to walk out after dark; and they never think of sleeping abroad, even at the house of their father or mother, unless the husband is with them. They therefore have seldom an opportunity of acting improperly. The father, mother, and whole family, also consider themselves disgraced by the bad conduct of a daughter or sister. And as, by the laws of England, a man may beat his wife with a stick which will not endanger the breaking of a limb, or may confine her in a room, the women dare not even give their tongues too much liberty. If, notwithstanding all these restraints, a woman should be so far lost to all sense of shame as to commit a disgraceful action, she is for ever after shunned by all her relations, acquaintances, and every lady of respectability. Her husband is also authorized by law to take away all her property and ornaments, to debar her from the sight of her children, and even to turn her out of the house; and if proof can be produced of her misconduct, he may obtain a divorce, by which she is entirely separated from him, and loses all her dower, and even her marriage portion. From what has been stated, it is evident that the English women, notwithstanding their apparent liberty, and the politeness and flattery with which they are addressed, are, by the wisdom of their lawgivers, confined in strict bondage: and that, on the contrary, the Mohammedan women, who are prohibited from mixing in society, and are kept concealed behind curtains, but are allowed to walk out in veils, and to go to the baths, and to visit their fathers and mothers and even female acquaintances, and to sleep abroad for several nights together, are much more mistresses of their own conduct, and much more liable to fall into the paths of error.

Translated by Charles Stewart, 2nd edn. London: Longman, Hurst, Rees, Orme & Brown, 1814, II, 27–31

DOCUMENT 11 ROBERT GEORGE HOBBES, 'CALCUTTA', 1851

The Eurasians or persons of mixed Indian-European ancestry, constituted one of the most marginalized communities in British India. In this extract, the prevailing prejudices against them are made clear, and as the author implies, part of the stigma that attached to them was due to so many of them being descended from the Portuguese, thereby bringing religion as well as race into the discussion.

They are generally the descendants of European fathers by native mothers. The great majority of them are of Portuguese, many of British, and some of French extraction. Altogether they form a community by themselves, as distinct from the European society around them as from the Hindoos and

Mahomedans. They do not travel, here they live and multiply, marrying generally among themselves. As they are daily increasing in number, they will, of course, in time become so numerous as to consider themselves a nation, and to demand a place in history. Should such, however, be the case, I do not think they will occupy a very high position in the scale of nations. Great talent (I will not mention genius), and sterling abilities seem very scarce amongst them. They devote no attention to the cultivation of arts, they manifest no zeal in the pursuits of science, no independence, no brotherly feeling towards each other. The females, at best, receive but a superficial education, it generally extending only to reading, writing, and the mechanical performance of music, dancing, and ornamental needlework, and in none of these do they show any extraordinary skill. As girls they are flirts and coquettes, as women they are vain, idle and slovenly. Let me be candid however. I have found among the Eurasians men possessing a versatility of talent that would do honour to any of our own countrymen, and females adorned with every grace and accomplishment. But such characters are very, very scarce.

Bentley's Miscellany 30 (1851): 368

DOCUMENT 12   **EDMUND BURKE SPEECH TO THE HOUSE OF LORDS ON THE OPENING OF WARREN HASTINGS' IMPEACHMENT TRIAL, 15 FEBRUARY 1788**

The prolonged impeachment of Warren Hastings has long occupied a prominent place in the historiography of British India. While much of this was undoubtedly due to the important issues which were raised by the trial, including detailed discussions over the rights and responsibilities of the conquering power, the rhetorical skills, not to mention rhetorical excesses, of Edmund Burke and the alarm he raised over the likelihood that Indian money and Indian values would corrupt Britain unless stopped ensured an even more attentive audience.

We have not chosen to bring before you a poor, puny, trembling delinquent, misled perhaps by the example of those who ought to have kept him in awe, and afterwards oppressed by their power in order to make his punishment the means of screening the greater offences of those that were above him. We have not brought before your Lordships one of those poor, obscure, offenders, in an inferior position, who, when his insignificance and weakness is weighed against the power of the prosecution, gives even to public justice something of the appearance of oppression. No, my Lords, we have brought before your Lordships the first man in rank, authority and station; we have brought before you the head, the chief, the captain-general in iniquity; one in whom all the frauds, all the peculations, all the violence, all the tyranny in India are embodied, disciplined and arrayed. . . . It is not from this Country or the other, from this district or the other, that relief is applied for, but from whole tribes of suffering nations, various descriptions of men, differing in language, in manners and in rights, men separated by every means from you. However, by the providence of God, they are come here to supplicate justice at your Lordship's Bar; and I hope and trust that there will be no rule, formed upon municipal maxims, which will prevent the Imperial justice which you owe to the people that call to you from all parts of a great disjointed empire. Situated as this Kingdom is – an object, thank God, of envy to the rest of the world for its greatness and power – its conduct, in that very elevated situation to which it has arisen, will undoubtedly be scrutinized. It is well known that great wealth has poured into this country from India; and it is no derogation to us to suppose the possibility of being corrupted by that by which great Empires have been corrupted, and by which assemblies almost as respectable and venerable as Lordships' have been known to be indirectly shaken. My Lords, when I say that forty millions of money have come from India to England, we ought to take great care that corruption does not follow . . . There is not honest emolument, in much the greater part of it [the East India Company], correspondent to the nature and answerable to the expectations of the people who serve. There is an unbounded licence in almost all other respects: and, as one of the honestest and ablest servants of the Company said to me, that it resembled the service of the Mahrattas – little pay, but unbounded licence to plunder. This is the pay of the Company's Service, a service opened to all dishonest emolument, shut up to all things that are honest and fair.

In P.J. Marshall, ed., *The Writings and Speeches of Edmund Burke: Volume VI. India: the Launching of the Hastings Impeachment, 1786–1788.* Oxford: Oxford University Press, 1991

DOCUMENT 13   **ARTHUR WELLESLEY, DUKE OF WELLINGTON, 'MEMORANDUM ON THE TREATY OF BASSEIN', 1804**

The Treaty of Bassein was intended by the then governor-general, Richard Wellesley, to provide a framework within which relations between the British and the Maratha confederacy could be put upon a more stable foundation. In this memorandum, Arthur Wellesley, the future Duke of Wellington and brother to the governor-general, takes issue with the assumptions underpinning the treaty, namely that Indian rulers subscribed to the same political principles and guidelines as did Europeans. Consequently, Arthur Wellesley did not hold much hope for a European-style balance of power for the subcontinent.

The Asiatic governments do not acknowledge and hardly know of such rules and systems (balance of power). Their governments are arbitrary, the objects of their policy are always shifting; they have no regular established system, the effect of which is to protect the weak against the strong: on the contrary, the object of each of them separately, and all of them collectively, is to destroy the weak; and if by chance they should, by a sense of common danger, be induced for a season to combine their efforts for their mutual defence, the combination lasts only so long as it is attended with success, the first reverse dissolves it; and at all events, it is dissolved long before the danger ceases, the apprehension of which originally caused it. . . . These observations apply to the government of the Mahrattas more than to any other of the Asiatic governments. Their schemes and systems of policy are the wildest of any. They undertake expeditions, not only without viewing their remote consequences upon other states, or upon their own, but without considering more than the chance of success of the immediate expedition in contemplation. . . . The picture above drawn of the state of politics among Asiatic powers proves that no permanent system can be adopted, which will preserve the weak against the strong, and will keep all for any length of time in their relative situations, and the whole in peace; excepting there should be one power which, either by the superiority of its strength, its military system, or its resources, shall preponderate and be able to protect all.

> In Arthur Wellesley and John Gurwood, *Selections from*
> *the Dispatches and General Orders of Field Marshal*
> *the Duke of Wellington; by Lieut. Col. Gurwood*. London:
> John Murray, 1841, 189–90

DOCUMENT 14   EDITORIAL ON THE FRONTIERS OF BRITISH INDIA

A major problem facing the British in India was where they should establish their western boundaries as the social and political realities of the area did not correspond to the natural frontiers offered by rivers or mountain ranges, and as illustrated in this editorial, there was a constant tendency to push the boundary outwards in the hopes of acquiring some stability.

The truth is we have power in abundance. We can conquer as we please, but we do not care to occupy, and we cannot civilize. The difficulty is in circumscribing our empire, not in extending it. We want a clear frontier and a friendly neighbour, and if we could find such blessings even on the borders of Persia, we could easily enough march to seek them. Whether we have lately taken judicious steps in this direction may be a doubtful question. We confess our belief that we have paid dearly for Scindian gains – for the sorry substitution of the Indus for the desert as our safest frontier.

> *The Times*, 12 December 1846

BANKIMCANDRA CHATTERJI: ANANDAMATH, 1905

In this excerpt from Chatterji's Anandamath, *first published in 1882, one of the most significant Indian literary works of the nineteenth century, the sufferings endured by the people of Bengal during the famine of 1769–70 are poignantly depicted.* Anandamath *helped forge a sense of shared suffering at the hands of a foreign and oppressive ruler and contributed to the development of early Hindu nationalism. The words of* Bande Mataram, *India's national anthem, were taken from this book.*

In 1174 there was a bad harvest. So food became a little dear in 1175. The people were in distress but the State realized its dues to the last penny. Having paid down the royal dues, the poor people satisfied themselves with but one good meal a day and struggled on. There was a good shower during the rains of 1175 and the people thought with joy that the gods had perhaps smiled on them. The shepherd began his carol again and the peasant's wife began to tease her spouse for the silver armlet. Suddenly the gods turned angry in Aswin [September–October], for there was not a drop of rain in that month and the crops in the field dried up into hay. Those who reaped a harvest at all had their crop bought up by the State for the support of its army. The people therefore starved. At first they had one meal a day, then they went on half rations, and then starved the whole day. The small Chaitra [March–April] harvest that they gathered was not enough for anybody. But Mahommed Reza Khan, the officer in charge of the State revenue, thought he would be a favourite of the authorities by a stroke at this time, and forthwith enhanced the assessment by ten per cent. There was a howl of grief all over Bengal.

First, people began to beg. But soon there was none to give alms; they began to starve. Then they began to suffer from diseases. They sold their cattle, sold their ploughs, ate up the seed grains, sold their houses and their holdings, and at last their daughters and sons and wives. Then there could not be found buyers of men, everybody wanted to sell. They then fed on leaves, grass and weeds for want of other food; the lower classes and wild tribes fed on dogs, mice and cats. Many fled and died of starvation away from their homes. Those who did not fly away died from starvation or from diseases brought on by eating unwholesome food. Diseases had a jolly time of it. Fever, cholera and small-pox prevailed, particularly the last. People died in every house from small-pox. There was none to touch them, treat them, or give them a drink. No one looked at any body else. No one removed the dead. The fairest bodies lay down to rot in the mansions. When small-pox once made its appearance in a house, the householders instantly took to flight, leaving the patient behind.

The Abbey of Bliss: A Translation of Bankim Chandra Chatterjee's Anandamath.
Calcutta: T.C. Dass, 1905, 4–5

ROMESH CHANDRA DUTT (ROMESH CHUNDER DUTT) *THE ECONOMIC HISTORY OF INDIA UNDER EARLY BRITISH RULE*, 1906

This extract from Dutt's Economic History *is characteristic of late nineteenth-century liberal nationalist thought: it is both highly critical of the shortcomings of British rule, particularly in its failure to live up to its economic responsibilities, while at the same time upholding several of the fundamental tenets of western civilization, particularly its emphasis on science, reason and education.*

Englishmen can look back on their work in India, if not with unalloyed satisfaction, at least with some legitimate pride. They have conferred on the people of India what is the greatest human blessing – Peace. They have introduced Western education, bringing an ancient and civilized nation in touch with modern thought, modern sciences, modern institutions and life. They have built an Administration, which, though it requires reform with the progress of the times, is yet strong and efficacious. They have framed wise laws, and have established Courts of Justice, the purity of which is as absolute as in any country on the face of the earth. These are the results which no honest critic of British work in India regards without high admiration.

On the other hand, no open-minded Englishman contemplates the material condition of the people of India under British rule with equal satisfaction. The poverty of the Indian population at the present day is unparalleled in any civilized country; the famines which have desolated India within the last quarter of the nineteenth century are unexampled in their intent and intensity in the history of ancient or modern times. By a moderate calculation, the famines of 1877 and 1878, of 1889 and 1892, of 1897 and 1900, have carried off fifteen millions of people. The population of a fair-sized European country has been swept away from India within twenty-five years. A population equal to half that of England has perished in India within a period which men and women, still in middle age, can remember.

From the Rise of the British Power in 1757 to the Accession of Queen Victoria in 1837,
2nd edn. London: K. Paul, Trench, Trübner, 1906, vii–viii, xix–xx

A NATIVE, *NIL DURPAN: THE INDIGO PLANTER'S MIRROR*, 1860(?)

Nil Durpan (Nil Darpan), *a Bengali play about the horrific conditions under which indigo cultivators worked and which in turn led to a series of uprisings in Bengal and Bihar, caused a sensation when Anglo-Indian society came to know of it. The Reverend Long translated the play into English and had it published; he was subsequently charged with libel and imprisoned for one month. Not all of officialdom supported the court's actions: the Viceroy and the Secretary of State for India both felt that Long had been unjustly punished and in their private correspondence evinced some sympathy for the sufferings of the indigo cultivators.*

Oh, ye indigo planters! your malevolent conduct has brought a stain upon the English nation, which was so graced by the ever memorable names of Sidney, Howard, Hall and other great men. Is your desire for money so very powerful that through the instigation of that vain wealth, you have engaged to make holes like rust in the long acquired and pure fame of the British people? Abstain now from that unjust conduct through which you are raising immense sums as your profits; and then the poor people with their families will be able to spend their days in ease. You are now-a-days purchasing lands with 100 rupees by expending only 10; – but you well know what great troubles the *ryot*s are suffering from that. Still you are not willing to make that known, being entirely given up to the acquisition of money. You say that some amongst you give donations to schools, and also medicine in time of need, – but the planters' donations to schools are more odious than the application of the shoe for the destruction of the milch cow, and their grants of medicine are like unto mixing the inspissated milk in the cup of poison. If the application of a little turpentine after being beat by shamchand (leather whip) be forming a dispensary, then it may be said that in every factory there is a dispensary.

A Drama, Translated from the Bengali. Edinburgh: Myles Macphail, 1860(?), 3

DOCUMENT 18   JAMES MILL, *THE HISTORY OF BRITISH INDIA,* 1818

Mill's History of British India *was much more than simply a narrative of developments in India; instead, and not surprisingly given Mill's standing as a political philosopher, it provided one of the first sustained statements of what would become known as the Anglicist position on India which crudely put argued that there was little to value within India's cultural and intellectual traditions. Was India to progress, it could only do so by shedding itself of its irrational and superstitious traditions. It was on the strength of his* History *that James Mill was hired by the East India Company, eventually retiring as Examiner, the senior-most position in London.*

We have seen, in the comparisons adduced to illustrate the state of civilization among the Hindus, that the nations, in the western parts of Asia; the Persians, the Arabians, and even the Turks; possessed a degree of intellectual faculties rather higher than the nations situated beyond them toward the East; were rather less deeply involved in the absurdities and weaknesses of a rude state of society; had in fact attained a stage of civilization, in some little degree, higher than the other inhabitants of that quarter of the globe. This is a statistical fact, to which it is not probable that much contradiction will hereafter be applied. . . . The Mahomedans were exempt from the institution of caste; that institution which stands a more effective barrier against the welfare of human nature than any other institution which the workings of caprice and of selfishness have ever produced. . . . The laws of the Hindus, we have already seen, are such as could not originate in any other than one of the weakest conditions of the human intellect; and, of all the forms of law known to the human species, they exhibit one of the least capable of producing the benefits which it is the end and the only consequence of law to ensure. On the present occasion, it appears sufficient to say, that even those who make the highest demand upon us for admiration of the poetry of the Hindus, allow, as Sir William Jones, for example, that the poetry of the Persians is superior. Compare the Mahabart [*Mahabharata*], the great narrative poem of the Hindus, with the Shah Namah [*Shah Nama*], the great narrative poem of the Persians; the departure from nature and probability is less wild and extravagant; the incidents are less foolish; the fictions are more ingenious; all to a degree, in the work of the Mahomedan author, than in that of the Hindu.

Edited by William Thomas, abridged edn. Chicago: University of Chicago Press,
1975, 299–300, 305, 310, 329

DOCUMENT 19   **ROSALIND AND MADELINE DUNLOP, *THE TIMELY RETREAT; OR A YEAR IN BENGAL BEFORE THE MUTINIES*, 1858**

While most published travelogues of India played up the sensational, the picturesque or the romantic, a number of travelogues written by British women in India, such as this one composed by two sisters in the years just before the Indian Mutiny, took it upon themselves to describe their often trying, sometimes dangerous and all too commonly monotonous lives, thereby contributing to some of the stock stereotypes of the English woman or memsahib in India.

It is nearly impossible to give people at home the slightest idea of the monotonous sameness of a lady's life in the hot weather even in a large station; but I can never hope to describe anything like the utterly dreary existence of ladies at an out-station (as I have heard it done), the complete stagnation of all amusement, almost of employment, the utter lassitude and exhaustion of the body, and the perfect depression and prostration of the mental energies. Suppose you are (as is often the case) the only lady at the station, your husband goes out to office about ten o'clock. Now, if you have any children, fortunate, indeed, are you; those untiring little mortals will always give full employment to any one who chooses to take much trouble about them. Their powers of life are fresh and young; there is an unending spring of vital energy about them, which even the hot weather cannot subdue. In the simple fact of dressing them up for their morning and evening drives, the languid mother may find some occupation and exercise for her taste at least; but supposing you have no children, or they are in England, what remains to be done? Literally nothing. Until about seven o'clock you know no single event (with the exception of tiffin [lunch]) will occur to break the monotony of the day. The piano is too much out of tune to be bearable; besides, the exertion of touching it is too great; you have written up all your correspondence; you have read all the amusing books in the house, and have not energy enough to begin any others; you cannot possibly sleep any more; if you look out of the window, the glare blinds you; and if you could bear it, you would see nothing – no moving creature to break the stillness. If a woman has a highly-cultivated mind, and many resources within herself, she may battle more bravely against the adverse circumstances around her; but when failing health is added to all the rest, there are few people who will not at least deteriorate very much, if they do not altogether succumb. When seven o'clock comes at last, and you get into the carriages, there are, perhaps, only two drives to choose from, both of which you know so well and are so wearied of. When you are out you see no one, save two or three exhausted gentlemen, driven out by ennui to take a breath of air, such as it is, hot and glowing. You return to find your husband too tired with his day's work to speak, almost to listen to you. . . . Probably military men suffer almost as much from ennui as ladies do; but then they have generally some kind of mess to resort to, and a billiard table, as well as the solace of smoking. Besides, I naturally pity my own sex the most.

2nd edn. London: Richard Bentley, 1858, I, 206–9

DOCUMENT 20   MACAULAY, 'WARREN HASTINGS', 1898

One of the most persistent British caricatures of India is that of the effete, clever but untrustworthy Bengali. In this extract from his essay on Warren Hastings, the noted historian, law reformer and essayist Thomas Babington Macaulay echoes these stereotypes and like many others attributes this lack of 'manly vigour' to Bengal's social and physical geography.

The physical organization of the Bengalee is feeble even to effeminacy. He lives in a constant vapour bath. His pursuits are sedentary, his limbs delicate, his movements languid. During many ages he has been trampled upon by men of bolder and more hardy breeds. Courage, independence, veracity, are qualities to which his constitution and situation are equally unfavourable.

His mind bears a singular analogy to his body. It is weak even to helplessness, for purposes of manly resistance; but its suppleness and its tact move the children of sterner climates to admiration not unmingled with contempt. . . . Large promises, smooth excuses, elaborate tissues of circumstantial falsehood, chicanery, perjury, forgery, are the weapons, offensive and defensive, of the people of the Lower Ganges.

The Works of Lord Macaulay: Essays and Biographies, Volume III.
London: Longmans, Green & Co., 1898, 425

DOCUMENT 21   RAMMOHUN ROY, 'SUTTEE AS A RELIGIOUS RITE', 1830

In taking action against sati *or the practice of burning widows on their husband's funeral pyres, the British sought expert testimony to the effect that* sati *was not a religious rite expressly required by sacred Hindu texts. Much of this was produced by the noted Bengali reformer and social activist, Rammohun Roy, whose writings were used to counter those who defended the rite on religious grounds.*

The first point to be ascertained is, whether or not the practice of burning widows alive on the pile and with the corpse of their husbands, is imperatively enjoined by the Hindu religion. To this question, even the staunch advocates for concremation [Suttee] must reluctantly give a negative reply, and unavoidably concede the practice to the option of widows. This admission on their part is owing to principal considerations, which it is now too late for them to feign to overlook. First, because Manu in plain terms enjoins a widow to 'continue till death forgiving all injuries, performing austere duties, avoiding every sensual pleasure, and cheerfully practicing the incomparable rules of virtue which have been followed by such women as were devoted to one only husband'. So Yajnavalkya inculcates the same doctrine: 'A widow shall live under care of her father, mother, son, brother, mother-in-law, father-in-law, or uncle; since, on the contrary, she shall be liable to reproach. Secondly, because an attempt on the part of the advocates for concremation to hold out the act as an incumbent duty on widows, would necessarily bring a stigma upon the character of the living widows, who have preferred a virtuous life to concremation, as charging them with a violation of the duty said to be indispensable'.

Selected Works of Raja Rammohun Roy. New Delhi: Government of India, Ministry of
Information and Broadcasting, Publications Division, 1977, 158

DOCUMENT 22   TAYLOR, 'ON THE THUGS', 1833

British fascination with the gangs of murderers who allegedly killed out of a sense of religious duty was triggered by graphic and often melodramatic accounts of their activities. This is one of the earliest accounts and was writ-ten by Philip Meadows Taylor, then serving in the territories of the Nizam of Hyderabad, close to the areas where the thugs were thought to be most active. Taylor would go on to write a number of novels set in nineteenth-century India, including Confessions of a Thug, *a fictionalized memoir of a thug leader that would become a best-seller in Britain, numbering Queen Victoria as one of its biggest fans.*

The Thugs form a perfectly distinct class of persons, who subsist almost entirely upon the produce of the murders they are in the habit of committing. They appear to have derived their denomination from the practice usually adopted by them of decoying the persons they fix upon to destroy, to join their party; and then taking advantage of the confidence they endeavour to inspire, to strangle their unsuspecting victims. . . . To trace the origins of this practice would now be a matter of some difficulty for if the assertions of the Thugs themselves are entitled to any credit, it has been in vogue from time immemorial; and they pretend that its institution is coeval with the creation of the world. Like most other inhuman practices, the traditions regarding it are mixed up with tales of Hindoo superstition; and the Thugs would wish to make it appear that, in immolating the numberless victims that yearly fall by their hands, they are only obeying the injunctions of the deity of their wor-ship, to whom they are offering an acceptable sacrifice. . . . The Thugs have in use among them, not exactly a language of their own, but they have sets of slang terms and phrases which give them the means of holding a conversation with persons of their own class, without any chance of being understood by the uninitiated. . . . To facilitate their plan of operations, the Thugs have established a regular system of intelligence and communication throughout the countries they have been in the practice of frequenting, and they have become acquainted, with astonishing celerity, with proceedings of their com-rades in all directions. . . . The peculiar designation by which they are known is a point in which the Thugs are particularly tenacious, and they attach an importance and even respectability to their profession, that they say no other class of delinquents is entitled to. The denomination of thief is one that is par-ticularly obnoxious to them, and they never refrain from soliciting the erasure of the term, and the substitution of that of Thug.

New Monthly Magazine 38 (1833): 277–8, 285

DOCUMENT 23   MACAULAY, 'MINUTE ON INDIAN EDUCATION',
2 FEBRUARY 1835

T.B. Macaulay's Minute on Indian Education, *written during his brief tenure as law member on the Governor-General's council, is arguably the most famous expression of British disdain for traditional Indian learning. In this extract, the reasons why English language and English education must be introduced into India are made clear: only then can Britain be assured that it has the trustworthy Indian partners needed if India is to progress.*

All parties seem to be agreed on one point, that the dialects commonly spoken among the natives of this part of India contain neither literary nor scientific information, and are, moreover, so poor and rude that, until they are enriched from some other quarter, it will not be easy to translate any valuable work into them. . . . We must at present do our best to form a class who may be interpreters between us and the millions whom we govern; a class of persons, Indian in blood and colour, but English in taste, in opinions, in morals, and in intellect. To that class we may leave it to refine the vernacular dialects of the country, to enrich those dialects with terms of science borrowed from the Western nomenclature, and to render them by degrees fit vehicles for conveying knowledge to the great mass of the population.

> In G.M. Young, ed., *Speeches of Lord Macaulay with His Minute on Indian Education.*
> Oxford: Oxford University Press, 1935, 348, 359

DOCUMENT 24   RAMMOHUN ROY IN *THE ATHAENAEUM*, 1833

Written shortly before his death, Rammohun Roy's retrospective on his early life details the reasons why he turned to western ideas and institutions in an effort to revitalize Indian society, even though this seriously strained relations with his family and friends.

When about the age of sixteen I composed a manuscript, calling in question the validity of the idolatrous system of the Hindus. This, together with my known sentiments on that subject, having produced a coolness between me and my immediate kindred, I proceeded on my travels, and passed through different countries, chiefly within, but some beyond, the bounds of Hindustan, with a feeling of great aversion to the establishment of British power in India. When I had reached the age of twenty, my father called and restored me to his favour; after which, I first saw, and began to associate with Europeans, and soon after made myself tolerably acquainted with their laws and forms of government. Finding them generally more intelligent, more steady, and moderate in their conduct, I gave up my prejudices against them, and became inclined in their favour: feeling persuaded that their rule, though a foreign yoke, would lead most speedily and surely to the amelioration of the native inhabitants. I enjoyed the confidence of several of them even in their public capacity. My continued controversies with the Brahmins on the subject of their idolatry and superstition, and my interference with their custom of burning widows, and other pernicious practices, revived and increased their animosity against me with renewed force; and, through their influence with my family, my father was again obliged to withdraw his countenance openly, though his limited pecuniary support was still continued to me. After my father's death I opposed the advocates of idolatry with still greater boldness; availing myself of the art of printing, now established in India. I published various works and pamphlets against their errors, in the native and foreign languages. This raised such a feeling against me that I was at least deserted by every person, except two or three Scotch friends, to whom, and the nation to which they belong, I always feel grateful. The ground which I took in all my controversies was not that of opposition to Brahmanism [Hinduism], but to a perversion of it; and I endeavoured to show that the idolatry of the Brahmins was contrary to the practice of their ancestors, and the principles of the ancient books and authorities, which they profess to revere and obey. Notwithstanding the violence of the opposition and resistance to my opinions, several highly respectable persons, both among my own relations and others, began to adopt the same sentiments.

5 October 1833, 666–7

DOCUMENT 25 **DAYANANDA SARASWATI RESPONDING TO THE QUESTION OF WHETHER OTHER REFORM MOVEMENTS LIKE THE BRAHMO SAMAJ ARE GOOD, 1875**

In the collection of essays later translated and published in English as The Light of Truth, *Dayananda Saraswati set forth many of the principles that would become the foundations of the Arya Samaj, a Hindu revivalist movement which contributed to the rise of Indian nationalism. Like the Brahmo Samaj, the Arya Samaj challenged many of the superstitious rites which had come to be associated with Hinduism, yet it differed fundamentally from the Brahmo Samaj in that it rejected what it saw as the latter's subservience to western ideas, values and practices.*

They are not good in all respects. How can the principles of these who are unaware of Vedic lore be all good. They saved many persons from the clutches of Christianity, they removed idolatry also to a certain extent, and they protected people from the snares of certain spurious scriptures. These are all good points. But they are lacking in patriotism. They have borrowed much from Christianity in their way of living. They have also changed the rules of marriage. Instead of praising their country and glorifying their ancestors, they speak ill of them. In their lectures they eulogize Christians and Englishmen. They do not even mention the names of old sages, Brahma etc. But they say

that there was never a learned man like the English people from the very creation of the world, that Indians have all along remained ignorant, and that
they never made any progress. . . . The Brahma Samajists and Prathana
Samajists [another reform society] call themselves educated, though they have
no knowledge of the literature of their own country, i.e. Sanskrta. No permanent sort of reform is expected from those who, in their pride for English
education, are ready to launch a new religion. They observe no restrictions on
interdining with Englishmen, Moslems and low class people. They are perhaps under the impression that they and their country would be regenerated
simply by removing the restriction of food and caste.

Swami Dayananda Saraswati and Ganga Prasad Upadhyaya, *The Light of Truth. English
Translation of Swami Dayananda's Satyartha Prakasha.* Allahabad: Kala Press, 1960, 548–9

DOCUMENT 26   **WILLIAM WILSON HUNTER, *ANNALS OF RURAL
BENGAL, 1897***

*The Santal Rebellion, described here by William Hunter, was one of many
local uprisings against colonial rule which have often been overshadowed by
the larger and more widespread revolts such as those which rocked India in
1857–58. And as Hunter makes explicit, pacification campaigns were ugly
and brutal affairs, ones which were very much at odds with the common practice of depicting colonial warfare in noble and romantic terms.*

The details of border warfare, in which disciplined troops mow down half-
armed peasants, are unpleasant in themselves, and afford neither glory to the
conquerors nor lessons in the military art. After a lapse of thirteen years, the
officers who reduced the Santals can hardly be brought to dwell minutely on
the operation. 'It was not war,' one of them said to me, 'it was execution'; we
had orders to go out whenever we saw the smoke of a village rising above the
jungle. The magistrate used to go with us. I surrounded the village with my
Sepoys, and the magistrate called upon the rebels to surrender. On one occasion the Santals, forty-five in number, took refuge in a mud house. The magistrate called on them to surrender, but the only reply was a shower of arrows
from the half-opened door. I said, 'Mr Magistrate, this is no place for you,'
and went up with my Sepoys, who cut a large hole through the wall. I told
the rebels to surrender or I should fire in. The door again half opened, and a
volley of arrows was the answer. A company of sepoys advanced, and fired
through the hole. I once more called on the inmates to surrender, while my
men reloaded. Again the door opened, and a volley of arrows replied. Some
of the Sepoys were wounded, the village was burning all round us, and I had
to give the men orders to do their work. At every volley we offered quarter;
and at last, as the discharge of arrows from the door slackened, I resolved to
rush in and save some of them alive, if possible. When we got inside, we found

only one old man, dabbled with blood, standing erect among the corpses. One of my men went up to him, calling him to throw away his arms. The old man rushed upon the Sepoy, and hewed him down with his battle-axe. If a single Englishman had been sent to them who understood their wrongs, and would have redressed them, they declared there would have been no war. . . . They were the most truthful set of men I ever met; brave to infatuation.

7th edn. London: Smith, Elder & Co., 1897, 247–8

DOCUMENT 27 SYED AHMED KHAN, *THE CAUSES OF THE INDIAN REVOLT*, 1873

Shortly after the Indian Mutiny had been suppressed, efforts at identifying the root causes began to point towards the Muslims of British India. While Syed Ahmed Khan's writings were not simply intended to deflect attention away from the Muslims, by emphasizing the multi-faceted nature of the revolt, and the many and diverse grievances at work, his writings helped to strengthen the case for not treating the events of 1857–58 as either simply a mutiny by discontented soldiers or a cunning conspiracy hatched by disgruntled Muslim nobles.

The primary causes of rebellion are, I fancy, everywhere the same. It invariably results from the existence of a policy obnoxious to the dispositions, aims, habits, and views, of those by whom the rebellion is brought about. From this it follows that widely spread disaffection cannot spring from any solitary or local cause. Universal rebellion must rise from universal grounds for discontent or from streams, deriving from many different sources, but finally merging into one wide-spreading turbulent water. As regards the Rebellion of 1857, the fact is that for a long period, many grievances had been rankling in the hearts of the people. In course of time, a vast store of explosive material had been collected. It wanted but the application of a match to light it, and that match was applied by the Mutinous army.

Benares: Benares Medical Hall Press, 1873, 2–3

DOCUMENT 28 EDITORIAL ON NEWS FROM INDIA, 1857

When news of the massacre of European women and children at Kanpur reached Britain, the demands for vengeance drowned out the voices of those who were urging restraint. Even The Times, *which had hitherto been quite moderate in tone, urged revenge.*

We trust that England will spare no cost of men or of money to vindicate justice and humanity upon the person of this savage [Nana Sahib] . . .

Extraordinary crimes require extraordinary penalties; and, if we mean to sustain the British rule or human nature itself, in any wholesome sense of that term, in Hindostan, we must make a signal example of the men who have offered these affronts upon it. We occasionally hear whispers about cheap sentiments of mercy and pity for these men. Whatever we may desire for their souls, it is a plain matter of business what we have to do with their bodies, and not only India, but the world, will be intolerable if we neglect our duty to them. Nothing else will tell on the Mahomedan or the Hindoo. For our religion, for our teaching and preaching, they have an utter contempt. Fortunately they understand what it is to be hung, and have a particular objection to it. Indeed, we have heard lately some earnest remonstrances against the application of this process to persons so keenly sensitive of its disgrace. This renders it particularly adapted for the purpose.

The Times, 18 November 1857

DOCUMENT 29 BRITISH TREATMENT OF INDIANS, LORD ELGIN TO CHARLES WOOD, 22 JUNE 1862

The higher ranks of the British administration in India had long been critical of the casual brutality with which many Britons in India treated their servants or other Indians they encountered. The level of violence surged in the years after the Indian Mutiny, and in this letter the Viceroy complains of the difficulty of holding Europeans accountable in such a climate of racial hostility.

I have had this week another painful matter to deal with. A man of the name Rudd, a soldier who had obtained his discharge in order to accompany an officer of the name of Jellico to Australia, killed a native in the Punjaub some months ago under the following circumstances – he was desired by Jellico (who must be a very unprincipled man to judge by the evidence which he gave in the trial) to procure a sheep for him. He went to a native from whom he appears to have procured sheep before, and took one. The native protested against his taking this particular sheep because it was with lamb, but said he might take any other from the flock. Rudd paid no heed to this remonstrance, put the sheep on the back of another native and marched off. The owner followed, complaining and protesting. On this Rudd first fired two barrels over his head, then threw stones at him, and finally went into the house, brought out another gun, fired at him, and killed him on the spot. Beyond imploring that his sheep might be returned to him, it does not appear that the native did anything at all to provoke this proceeding. . . . The trial came on a few days ago, and the jury, much to their honour, found the prisoner guilty. On this an agitation was got up to obtain a commutation of the sentence of death which had been passed by the judge. . . . The verdict was clearly borne out by the evidence. The sentence was in accordance with law, and the judge, to whom I referred, had no reason to question it. The decision of the Gov Gen in Council was, that the law must take its course, and it was conveyed to the petitioners in a letter of which I enclose the copy. It is true that this murder was not committed with previous preparation and deliberation. It had not therefore this special quality of aggravation. But it was marked by an aggravation of its own, not less culpable, and unfortunately only too frequently characteristic of the homicides perpetrated by Europeans on natives in this country. It was committed in wanton recklessness, almost without provocation, under an impulse which would have been resisted if the life of the victim had been estimated at the value of that of a dog. Any action on my part which would have seemed to sanction this estimate of the value of native life would have been attended by the most pernicious consequences. It is bad enough as it is. The other day a station master somewhere up country, kicked a native who was, as he says, milking a goat belonging to the former. The native fell dead, and the local paper without a word of commiseration for the victim or his family, complains of the hardship of compelling the station master to go to Calcutta in this warm weather to have the case inquired into. Other instances in which natives have died from the effect of personal chastisement administered by Europeans have occurred since I have been here. I have gone at some length into this case, both because you may hear of it, and also because it exemplifies what is really our greatest source of embarrassment in this country – the extreme difficulty of administering equal justice between natives and Europeans. Indeed, I apprehend that the brutalities of low class Europeans are too much for the stomach of many even of those who would go great lengths in asserting Anglo-Saxon immunities and superiority.

MSS Eur F83/3, Elgin Papers, Oriental and India Office Collections, British Library

DOCUMENT 30   TREVELYAN, *THE COMPETITION WALLAH*, 1866

Trevelyan has long been thought to exemplify the ideals of the liberal-minded, reform-oriented, and public-spirited colonial official popularized by Victorian defenders of empire. Yet as this excerpt demonstrates, Trevelyan believed that the differences between the British and their Indian subjects were so substantial that it would be some time before there could be anything approaching genuine dialogue and effective partnership.

There is something very interesting in the first railway journey in Bengal. Never was I so impressed with the triumphs of progress, the march of mind. In fact, all the usual common-places genuinely filled my soul. Those two thin strips of iron, representing as they do the mightiest and most fruitful conquest of science, stretch hundreds and hundreds of miles across the boundless

Eastern plains – rich, indeed, in material products, but tilled by a race far below the most barbarous of Europeans in all the qualities that give good hope for the future of a nation. . . . When but seven years have passed since such a mine [the mutiny] lay beneath our feet unheeded and unknown, we should be slow to affirm that we understand the feelings and character of the people of India. Their inner life still remains a sealed book to us. Certain it is that we have a very vague notion of the estimation in which they hold us. It is hardly possible for a man brought up amidst European scenes and associations to realize the idea conceived of him and his countrymen by a thorough-bred Hindoo. On the one hand, the natives must acknowledge our vast superiority in the arts of war and government. Our railways, and steam-ships, and Armstrong guns are tangible facts which cannot be slighted. They must be perfectly aware that we have conquered them, and are governing them in a more systematic and downright manner than they have ever been gov-erned before. But, on the other hand, many of our usages must in their eyes appear most debased and revolting. Imagine the horror with which a punctil-ious and devout Brahmin cannot but regard a people who eat the flesh of cow and pig, and drink various sorts of strong liquors from morning till night. It is at least as hard for such a man to look up to us as his betters, morally and socially, as it would be for us to place amongst the most civilized nations of the world a population which was in the habit of dining on human flesh and intoxicating itself daily with laudanum and sal-volatile. . . .•The wide and radical difference between the views held by the respective races with regard to the weaker sex alone, forms a bar, at present insuperable, to any very familiar intercourse. We, who still live among the recollections and records of chivalry, horrify utilitarians by persisting in regarding women as goddesses. The Hindoos, who allow their sisters and daughters few or no personal rights – the Mahommedans, who do not even allow them souls – cannot bring them-selves to look upon women as better than playthings. . . . Among the num-berless symptoms of our national eccentricity, that which seems most extraor-dinary to a native is our submitting to be governed by a woman. . . . The longer a man lives in this country the more firmly convinced does he become that the amalgamation of the conquerors and the conquered is an idea impracticable, and, to use an odious word, Utopian. But this does not imply that, as time goes on, as the native becomes civilized, and the European humane and equitable, the two races should not live side by side with mutual sympathy and self-respect, and work together heartily for the same great ends.

2nd edn. London: Macmillan, 1866, 22, 345–6, 348, 349–50

DOCUMENT 31 **LORD LYTTON TO J. STRACHEY, 11 MAY 1876**

Despite the veneer of liberalism which often cloaked imperial activities in the nineteenth century, much of the ideology which sustained that empire was rooted in a very conservative reading of society. Nobody characterized this conservative ideology more fully than did Lord Lytton who, as this extract from one of his letters indicates, insisted that the only Indians who really mattered were the princes and other members of the traditional aristocracy.

Politically speaking, the Indian peasantry is an inert mass. If it ever moves at all, it will move in obedience, not to its British benefactors, but to its Native Chiefs and Princes, however tyrannical they may be. The only political representatives of native opinion are the Baboos [babu – derogatory term for a western-educated clerk], whom we have educated to write semi-seditious articles in the Native Press, and who really represent nothing but the social anomaly of their own position. . . . But the Indian Chiefs and Princes are not a mere noblesse. They are a powerful aristocracy. What is the trouble Ireland now gives us compared with the trouble she might give us if, at the head of the national Irish party, there were a really powerful national aristocracy? To secure completely, and efficiently utilize, the Indian aristocracy, is, I am convinced, the more important problem now before us . . .

MSS Eur E218/18, Oriental and India Office Collections, British Library, 149–50

DOCUMENT 32   DIGBY, *THE FAMINE CAMPAIGN IN SOUTHERN INDIA*, 1878

The tragic irony of a huge celebration being held at Delhi to honour the Queen at the same time as millions were starving because of a crippling famine in central and southern India was not lost on some commentators. A number of newspaper writers and pamphleteers struggled to bring attention to this situation, arguing, as shown here, that this reflected badly on both the intent and practice of colonial rule.

India is a land of startling contrasts, but extremes were never more vividly noted than in the scenes which were being witnessed on the plains of Delhi in the north, and in the districts in the south, in the early days of January 1877. The spectacular splendour of the Imperial Assemblage surpassed anything of the kind that the continent had ever known: the Field of the Cloth of Gold was not more magnificent. Similarly, while the assemblage was being held, but, owing to the tardiness with which returns are prepared and forwarded to headquarters, in a great measure unknown to those who were taking part in the ceremonies, – unequalled scenes of death and disaster were occurring south and west of the Kistna delta.

Whilst preparations were being made for the proclamation of Her Majesty the Queen of Great Britain as Empress of India, and whilst the ceremonies were actually in progress, 65,000 subjects of the Queen-Empress died of starvation and the diseases caused by insufficient nourishment, in the Madras Presidency alone. Thirteen thousand must similarly have perished in the province of Mysore, but no record of deaths month by month has been published; how many died in Bombay Presidency is unknown, for here, too, reticence was displayed respecting mortality whilst scarcity and want were prevalent.

London: Longmans, 1878, I, 45

DOCUMENT 33   'PETITION OF ENGLISHWOMEN IN INDIA' 1883

The proposal to allow Indian judges to try Europeans was forcefully rejected by Anglo-Indians on the grounds that Indian judges would then be in a position to abuse their authority. A critical argument in the agitation against Courtney Ilbert's efforts at legal reform was provided by English women who resurrected fears that stretch back to 1857 of the perils that faced English women should they be exposed to Indian males.

We would humbly submit that the position held by women in Native society is so entirely different from that held by their European sisters, and this difference so deeply affects all the relations of social and domestic life, and the customs, habits and feelings connected with those relations, that no native of India, however highly educated, can possess the knowledge or sympathy essential to a correct appreciation of the feelings and conduct of European women. But such a correct appreciation of the feelings and conduct of accused persons can alone qualify a judge to try them; and consequently the effect of the proposed change in the law would be to transfer the trial of European women in India to men who, by the force of circumstances, are incompetent to do them justice. . . . For the knowledge of the injury and of the dread with which we should regard it, would operate as a powerful incentive to any ill-disposed Natives to resort to false charges against us for the purposes of extortion, intimidation, and revenge; and this temptation would be increased by a belief in our helplessness before an alien tribunal, isolated, as we should in many cases be, from our natural protectors; unable, as we should be in the great majority of cases, to obtain the assistance of European counsel, and ignorant, as we should generally be, of the language in which the proceedings would be conducted.

In the Anglo-Indian Association, *The Ilbert Bill. A Collection of Letters, Speeches, Memorials, Articles, Etc.* London: W.H. Allen, 1883, 90–2

DOCUMENT 34   B. KRISHNA SINGH ON LORD RIPON'S POLICY, 1883

An important element in the emergence of Indian nationalism was the growing frustration many Indians felt, such as that expressed by the author quoted below, over the pronounced disjunction between the liberal values extolled by the British and their often arbitrary and illiberal actions. Anglo-Indian condemnations of Ilbert's legal reforms provided some of the most explicit examples of the hypocrisy which so thoroughly infused imperial rule.

The noisy section of non-official Englishmen in India, and their advocates in England, are carried away by imaginary fears, in supposing that the liberty of European British subjects in India is in imminent danger; and it is no wonder that, labouring under such wrong notions, they should toil and moil to protest against the bill. Nor is this all: vigorous oppositions have been organized, Defence Associations have been formed, subscriptions started, and memorials forwarded, with a view to oppose the Bill passing into law. But what appears to me really surprising, is that these men, who are in the habit of taking liberal views of things in their own country, and who generally preach the higher and nobler sentiments embodied in Christianity, should so forget themselves in vain excitement about a mere shadow. . . . English capitalists can never get on well, unless and until they cooperate with the children of the soil.

Observations on the Criminal Jurisdiction Bill. Bangalore: The Caxton Press, 1883, 2–3

DOCUMENT 35   RUDYARD KIPLING, 'FOR THE WOMEN', 1887

The conditions within which Indian women lived and died had commonly been used as a yardstick by which the virtues of western civilization could be measured. They also provided a rationale for colonial rule, and a number of the most publicized reform efforts were directed towards Indian women. By the latter half of the nineteenth century, plans for further reforms created unique opportunities for European women to participate in imperial activities, for social customs in India meant that western women could penetrate more deeply into domestic spaces than could European men.

Help here – and not for us the boon and not to us the gain;
Make room to save the babe from death, the mother from her pain.
Is it so great a thing we ask? Is there no road to find
When women of our people seek to help your womankind?

No word to sap their faith, no talk of Christ or creed need be,
But woman's help in woman's need and woman's ministry.
Such healing as the West can give, that healing may they win.
Draw back the purdah for their sake, and pass our women in!

Civil and Military Gazette, 18 February 1887, reprinted in Rudyard Kipling, *Early Verse.*
vol. 18, *The Writings in Prose and Verse of Rudyard Kipling.* London: Macmillan, 1900

DOCUMENT 36 TARABAI SHINDE AND THE CRITIQUE OF GENDER RELATIONS, 1882

The conviction of an upper-caste widow for infanticide prompted Tarabai Shinde to publish in 1882 a tract that was critical of the caste and gender conventions which currently prevailed. Yet she based her attack not so much on a blanket denunciation of Indian practices and conventions but rather the highly selective interpretation of religious and social customs by men which ensured the ongoing subordination of women.

In fact, it's you men and these worthless fads and fancies of yours that have wrecked all our own native ways of making a living, so our tradesmen and skilled craft people are all perishing of hunger. Our glory has all been driven away and Lakshmi [Hindu Goddess of Prosperity and Good Fortune], who all of you press to make her home in yours, she's seen these fads, these dirty defiling habits of yours and she's taken herself away now, on the road to a distant country. So I place this little book before you, so you might have some pity for women who are widows, and for the wives and children of these poor working folk. I'm doing it to make you men open your eyes and take a look at your country and have some pride in it, rather than each of you just abandoning the dharma [righteousness or moral code], habits and customs of his own country. I'm doing it out of the hope that you might stop treating all women as though they had committed a crime and making their lives a hell for it.

R.A. O'Hanlon, *Comparison between Women and Men: Tarabai Shinde and the Critique of Gender Relations in Colonial India*. Madras, Oxford University Press, 1994, 76–7

DOCUMENT 37 PANDITA SARASWATI RAMABAI, *THE HIGH-CASTE HINDU WOMAN*, 1887

Pandita Ramabai, a Brahmin widow who converted to Christianity, became one of the most widely known social activists who through her travels to Europe and America sought to bring attention to the conditions in which many Indian women lived. Her writings anticipated the maternal nationalism of some later nationalists by insisting that the health and the future of the nation could only be sustained if adequate support was given to women who were the custodians of the next generation.

Those who have done their best to keep women in a state of complete dependence and ignorance, vehemently deny that this has anything to do with the present degradation of the Hindu nation. . . . In the animal as well as in the vegetable kingdom, nature demands that all living beings shall freely comply with its conditions of growth or they cannot become that which they were originally designed to be. Why should any exception to this law be made for the purdah women? Closely confined to the four walls of their house, deprived throughout their lives of the opportunity to breathe healthy fresh air, or to drink in the wholesome sunshine, they become weaker and weaker from generation to generation, their physical statures dwarfed, their spirits crushed under the weight of social prejudices and superstitions, and their minds starved from absolute lack of literary food and of opportunity to observe the world. Thus fettered, in ninety cases out of a hundred, at the least calculation, they grow to be selfish slaves to their petty individual interests, indifferent to the welfare of their immediate neighbours, much more to the nation's well-being. How could these imprisoned mothers be expected to bring forth children better than themselves, for as the tree and soil are, so shall the fruit be. Consequently we see all around us in India a generation of men least deserving that exalted appellation. The doctrine of 'pre-natal influences' can nowhere be more satisfactorily proved than in India. The mother's spirits being depressed, and mind as well as body weakened by the monotony and inactivity of her life, the unborn child cannot escape the evil consequences. The men of Hindustan do not when babes, suck from the mother's breast, true patriotism and in their boyhood, the mother, poor woman, is unable to develop that divine faculty in them owing to her utter ignorance of the past and present conditions of her native land.

Philadelphia, 1887, 95–7

DOCUMENT 38   **DADABHAI NAOROJI'S PRESIDENTIAL ADDRESS TO THE SECOND MEETING OF THE INDIAN NATIONAL CONGRESS, CALCUTTA, 1886**

The first decade of the Indian National Congress was marked, at least offici-ally, by moderation and respectability. Its leaders were careful not to appear disloyal, and in fact as shown here by Naoroji's speech, they extolled the benefits that British rule brought to India. While some of this enthusiasm can undoubtedly be attributed to a desire not to antagonize the British, it also demonstrates just how thoroughly imbued were many of these earlier repre-sentatives with the values and ideals of western civilization.

The assemblage of such a Congress is an event of the utmost importance in Indian history. I ask whether in the most glorious days of Hindu rule, in the days of Rajahs like the great Vikram, you could imagine the possibility of a meeting of this kind, where even Hindus of all different provinces of the kingdom could have collected and spoken as one nation. Coming down to the later Empire of our friends, the Mahomedans, who probably ruled over a larger territory at one time than any Hindu monarch, would it have been, even in the days of the great Akbar himself, possible for a meeting like this to assemble composed of all classes and communities, all speaking one language, and all having uniform and high aspirations of their own?

Well, then what is it for which we are now met on this occasion? We have assembled to consider questions upon which depends our future, whether glorious or inglorious. It is our good fortune that we are under a rule which makes it possible for us to meet in this manner. (*cheers*) It is under the civilizing rule of the Queen and the people of England that we meet here together, hindered by none, and are freely allowed to speak our minds without the least fear and without the least hesitation. Such a thing is possible under British rule and British rule only. (*loud cheers*) I put the question plainly: Is this Congress a nursery for sedition and rebellion against the British Government; (*cries of no, no*) or is it another stone in the foundation of the stability of that Government? (*cries of yes, yes*) There could be but one answer, and that you have already given, because we are thoroughly sensible of the numberless blessings conferred upon us, of which the very existence of the Congress is a proof in a nutshell. (*cheers*) Were it not for these blessings of British rule I could not have come here, as I have done, without the least hesitation and without the least fear that my children might be robbed and killed in my absence; nor could you have come across every corner of the land, having performed, within a few days, journeys which in former days would have occupied as many months. (*cheers*) But there remains even greater blessings for which we have to be grateful. It is to British rule that we owe the education we possess. The people of England were sincere in their declarations made more than half a century ago that India was a sacred charge entrusted to their care by Providence, and that they were bound to administer it for the good of India, to the glory of their own name, and the satisfaction of God. (*prolonged cheering*)

In W.C. Bonnerjee, ed., *Indian Politics. [A Collection of Essays and Addresses.]* *With an Introduction by W.C. Bonnerjee*. Madras: G.A. Natesan & Co., 1898, 6–7

GLOSSARY

Adivasi Original or indigenous inhabitant of India, replaces the term tribal which earlier writers had used to identify communities that lived on the margins of settled society in India.

Anglo-Indian Term used throughout much of the nineteenth century to refer to Britons domiciled in India. It would later be used to identify persons of mixed ancestry, also known as Eurasians.

Arya Samaj Socio-religious reform movement started in 1875 by Dayananda Saraswati which was directed at restoring Hinduism to its Vedic roots and to reconverting Indians who had converted to other religions.

Babu Term of derision for western-educated Indians, typically assigned to Bengalis.

Banjaras Communities of nomadic grain and salt traders.

Bhadralok Respectable society in Bengal, roughly corresponding to the gentry, and usually but not always restricted to the high-caste Hindus.

Bhakti Devotional expression of faith in Hinduism.

Bhangra Traditional music and dance of Northern India (particularly the Punjab region) which has become popularized and integrated into popular dance music by Indian emigrants.

Brahmin The highest and purest of the four principal Hindu castes, customarily associated with the performance of priestly duties.

Brahmo Samaj A socio-religious movement founded in Bengal by Rammohun Roy that looked to a fusion of western and eastern ideas to cleanse Hinduism of idolatry and other practices that had led to deviations from the messages contained in the Vedas.

Caste Portuguese term for varna; the four classical social groupings as set forth in Hindu sacred texts.

Chauth Term for the customary Maratha demand for one-quarter of the land revenues from areas over which they claimed authority.

Dacoits Robbers operating in gangs.

Darbar Public audience, usually held to symbolize or celebrate royal authority.

Diwan Mughal term for the senior civil administrator in a province.

Diwani Civil authority, including the right to collect land revenues.

Doab Area of land lying between two rivers.

Ghats Mountain ranges along the western and eastern coasts; also steps or quays along river embankments.

Jagir The grant of rights to the revenues from a piece of land in return for service.

Jati Literally birth; in practice, sub-castes identified by occupation which serve as the basic social marker in daily life.

Khalsa   Army of the pure, armed brotherhood founded by the tenth and last guru of the Sikhs, Gobind Singh, in 1698.

Kshatriya   The second of the four Hindu castes, often refers to warriors.

Lascar   An Indian sailor.

Madrasa   Muslim school or place of learning.

Mansabdari   Administrative ranks within the Mughal Empire – in return for a particular rank, an office-holder would be expected to provide a specified number of troops in recognition of which he would be granted a *jagir*. *Mansabs* were not hereditary and were given at the discretion of the emperor.

Marathas   Ethnic and linguistically defined community in western and central India.

Maulvi   Muslim legal expert.

Mofussil   Rural areas, most commonly used in Bengal to distinguish the countryside from large urban centres such as Calcutta.

Munshi   Teacher or interpreter.

Nautch   Indian dance performance; also refers to Anglo-Indian public entertainment or ball.

Nawab   Muslim provincial governor, though the British often used this term and *raja* to refer indiscriminately to Indian princes and chiefs.

Orientalism   Initially used to refer to the study of the East, including India, and with a focus largely on religious and philosophical texts. More recently it has been used to refer to the knowledge that the West not only acquired of the East, but how that knowledge was used to ensure dominance by the West.

Pandit   Brahmin scholar.

Peshwa   Chief minister of the Maratha confederacy.

*Pindari*s   Military adventurers, many from Central Asia and the Middle East, active in Central India often in alliance with the Marathas.

Purdah   The practice of secluding women from public view.

Rani   Princess or queen.

Rupee   Principle currency in India, especially in the north. During much of this period, 1 rupee was worth 2 shillings.

Ryot (*ryat*)   Peasant or cultivator.

Ryotwari   Revenue system in which the peasant pays directly to the state.

Sanskrit   The sacred language of Hinduism which is part of the Indo-European language family.

Sati   Refers either to the widow who immolates herself on the funeral pyre of her husband, or to the act itself.

Sepoy   Indian soldiers, from the Persian word *sipahi* meaning foot soldier. Counterparts in the cavalry were termed *sowars*.

Shakti   Female power or regenerative force as understood within Hinduism.

Sikh   Literally a 'disciple' or follower of the teachings of Guru Nanak and his successors.

Sudra   Lowest of the four main caste groups, often associated with menial and service tasks.

Sufism   A mystical encounter or experience with Islam.

Swaraj   Home rule, self-government.

Taluqdar   Large rural magnates who served as intermediaries between the state and local society.

Thagi   (also thuggee). The ritual strangling and robbing of strangers.

Vaisya   The third of the four major castes within the Sanskrit tradition, usually associated with merchants and farmers.

Varna   Literally colour; in practice refers to the four principle social ranks in classical Hinduism: brahmin, kshatriya, vaisya, sudra.

Vedas   The four original sacred Hindu texts, the earliest of which has been dated back to around 1600 BCE.

Wahabism   Muslim revival movement that originated in Arabia in the eighteenth century which stressed a return to rigorous orthodoxy and a rejection of syncretic traditions.

Zamindar   Landlord or land-controller.

Zamindari   A revenue settlement in which taxes are the responsibility of landlords.

Zat   The numerical ranking that denoted status and entitlements within the Mughal aristocracy.

Ali, Haidar (d.1782) A Muslim military commander from northern India who sought service in southern India; he toppled the ruling Hindu dynasty in Mysore between 1761 and 1763 and very quickly built up a sophisticated administrative system and efficient army with which he was able to challenge British efforts at dominating southern India.

Banerjea, Surendranath (1848–1925) Born in Bengal and given a western education. Managed to overcome all the hurdles to become a member of the Indian Civil Service in 1871, only to be discharged three years later on rather spurious grounds. Turned his attention to education and political agitation and was an influential member of the Indian National Congress.

Bentinck, William (1774–1839) Military officer and governor of Madras (1803–07) and governor-general of India (1828–35). Autocratic by temperament, Bentinck brought to India a firm conviction of the need to modernize Indian society as well as improve British financial and civil administration. His term as governor-general saw the abolition of *sati*, the declaration of English as the sole official language of government administration, and a commitment to encourage western education.

Canning, Charles (1812–62) Appointed governor-general in 1856 in succession to Lord Dalhousie, and arrived in India just before the outbreak of the Indian Rebellion. His determined actions to limit retributions by the British antagonized much of the Anglo-Indian community and earned him the nickname of 'Clemency Canning'. In 1858 direct British rule replaced that of the East India Company and under the new regime Canning became the first Viceroy of India.

Chatterji, Bankimcandra (Chatterjee, Bankimchandra) (1838–94) Clerk in the Bengal Civil Service who was a major figure in the development of Bengali literature. His most famous novel, *Anandamath*, had as its major theme Mughal rule of Bengal, which was a metaphor for British conquest. The poem *Bande Mataram* became a rallying cry for later Indian nationalists.

Clive, Robert (1725–74) Sent to Madras as a clerk by the EIC in 1743. He was given a military commission during the struggles with the French and proved to be a very successful military commander. Promoted to lieutenant colonel in 1756 and shortly afterwards led the successful British mission to recapture Calcutta. Governor of Bengal 1758–60 and again in 1765–67. Became very wealthy on account of his Indian service and came to symbolize the excessive wealth which Company officials were suspected of acquiring through corrupt practices and extortion.

Cornwallis, Charles, 1st Marquess Cornwallis (1738–1805) Military officer, lord-lieutenant of Ireland and governor-general of India (1786–93). Served in the American Revolutionary War where he commanded the British troops when they were defeated at the Battle of Yorktown. Arrived in India determined to stamp out corruption and also ensure that property rights were upheld. He introduced a number of reforms intended to improve the behaviour of Company officials and was the prime mover behind the Permanent Settlement in Bengal in 1793 which was intended to turn *zamindar*s into English-style improving landlords. Cornwallis also oversaw military operations against Mysore in 1791–92. Was reappointed as governor-general of India in 1805 but died shortly after his arrival there.

Dalhousie, James Broun Ramsay, 1st Marquess of (1812–60) Appointed governor-general of India in 1848, Dalhousie came to India determined to modernize the colony through the introduction of new technologies like telegraphs and railways, and the imposition of direct British rule. Many of his reforms would later be judged to be at least partly responsible for the outbreak of the Indian Rebellion.

Hastings, Warren (1732–1818) Rose to the position of governor then governor-general (1772–85) after joining the Company's service in 1750. Demonstrated a deep interest in Indian culture and literature and actively patronized early Orientalists. His term as governor-general was marked by a series of challenges to British authority. The sometimes drastic actions he took to protect and consolidate Company rule led to a prolonged attempt at impeaching him, which began in 1786, with the trial beginning in 1788 and ending in his acquittal in 1795.

Jones, William (1746–94) Orientalist and judge. Jones was born in London and early on demonstrated a precocious talent for languages. In 1783, following a career that combined literary pursuits, political activity and work as a lawyer, Jones was sent to Bengal to serve as a judge. There, he was instrumental in founding the Asiatic Society of Bengal, and having learned Sanskrit, set about translating a number of the most important Hindu dramatic and legal texts into English. Jones was one of the first philologists to recognize that Sanskrit was related to Greek and Latin. He died in Calcutta just before his intended departure for Britain.

Khan, Syed Ahmed (1817–98) Born in Delhi, the son of an aristocratic Mughal family. He joined the East India Company, rising to the position of assistant magistrate and was stationed at Bijnor when the mutiny broke out. He managed to secure the safety of the small British population. He eventually retired in 1876 by which time he had become a judge in Benares. As an acknowledgement of his service, he was nominated to the central legislative council (1878–82). It was in those years that he paid a visit to Britain, and over the course of the seventeen months there he reached a number of conclusions as to the foundations of European ascendancy and how these might be used in India. Education was crucial, particularly scientific and technical learning offered where possible in vernacular languages so as to make it more accessible and meaningful for Indian students. A strong believer in reconciling Islam with western science and technology, he was instrumental in founding the Muhammadan Anglo-Oriental College at Aligarh in 1875.

Kipling, Rudyard (1865–1936) Born in Bombay, but educated in the UK, Kipling returned to India at the age of 17 when he began a career as a journalist. The stories and sketches that he wrote for the *Civil and Military Gazette* brought him fame at an early age, and many of these were collected and republished as books for a British audience. Although he is frequently criticized as an unquestioning defender of empire, scholars have recently begun to look more closely at the often ambivalent nature of his observations on India and of Britain's place there.

Lytton, Edward Bulwer, 1st Earl of Lytton (1831–91) Writer, diplomat and Viceroy of India (1876–80). Lytton arrived in India as one of Disraeli's favourites, and with a reputation based more on his literary activities than on public service though he had spent some time as a diplomat. A romantic at heart, Lytton instinctively sided with the traditional princes of India, had little time for western-educated Indians, and was committed to an aggressive foreign policy to maintain Britain's global stature.

Macaulay, Thomas Babington (1800–59) Writer and historian, Macaulay went to India in 1834 as the law member of the Governor-General's Council. Politically, Macaulay was a Whig and brought to India a conviction that India was in need of drastic reform. His Minute on Indian Education (1835) has become famous as exemplifying the increasingly negative views held by the British about the state of Indian culture and learning.

Nana Sahib (properly called Dhondu Pant) (d. c.1860) The heir of the last *peshwa*, Nana Sahib lived in exile in Kanpur. When the *peshwa* died in 1853, the allowances and perquisites which Nana Sahib expected would pass to him were discontinued. He unsuccessfully petitioned the British for their restoration, and when the Indian Rebellion broke out, he joined the rebels in Kanpur and declared himself to be the *peshwa*. He managed to escape when the city was recaptured by the British and is believed to have died in Nepal to which he had fled.

Naoroji, Dadabhai (1825–1917) One of the key figures in the early history of con-stitutional nationalism. Born in Bombay, Naoroji was a Zoroastrian, a religious community descended from migrants from Persia (and hence their more common name as Parsis). Naoroji was educated at Elphinstone College, one of the premier schools in India, where he would become professor of mathematics at the age of 27. He did not stay long, however, for he was drawn into commercial activity and left India in 1855 for London where he would combine business with the task of educating Britain about its responsibilities to its Indian subjects. Like many other nationalists of this era, Naoroji was a staunch loyalist (he was elected to the House of Commons as a Liberal in 1892). He subscribed to many of the ideals of British liberalism, and argued that India could benefit from the connection. Yet he was scathing in his attacks when the consequences of colonial rule fell short of their stated intent. For Naoroji, this was most evident in the ongoing drain of India's wealth to Britain. In 1901, he wrote *Poverty and un-British rule in India.*

Ramabai, Pandita Saraswati (1858–1922) Born into a Maratha Brahmin family, she was widowed at the age of 25. Accompanied by her young children she set off for England where she studied medicine and also converted to Christianity. She trav-elled to the USA where she was a popular speaker on the issue of social reform. Upon her return to India, she founded schools for the education of widows.

Rani Lakshmi Bai of Jhansi (d.1859) The widow of the Maratha ruler of Jhansi, she petitioned the British government in vain to allow her adopted son to succeed as ruler of Jhansi. She joined the rebels in 1857 and led troops against the British. Her death in battle turned her into a hero for later generations of Indian nationalists.

Roy, Rammohun (1772–1833) A Bengali Brahmin who was well versed in Sanskrit, Persian and English religious and philosophical writings, Roy championed the cause of social, political and religious reform in India through his writings, public lectures, and his contacts with British administrators. Was the founder of the Brahmo Samaj as well as of several newspapers in Bengal. Late in his life he travelled to Britain where he gave evidence before a Select Committee of Parliament called to consider the future of British rule in India. He spoke out in favour of the Reform Bill, and even thought about running for Parliament. He died in Bristol in 1833 and is buried in that city.

Saraswati, Dayananda (1824–83) Born into a moneylending family in Kathiawar, western India, Saraswati took up the life of wandering mendicant. He came to question traditional preoccupations with idol worship, sacrifice and contemplation and, observing the more aggressive and organized activities of Christian missionaries, began to develop a form of Hindu revivalism which had as its core a commitment to proselytism and a return to essentials. In 1875, he founded the Arya Samaj in Bombay but its activities came to focus on the Punjab.

Shinde, Tarabai (c.1850–1910) Born into a respectable Maratha family in a small town in Berar, central India. Her father was a member of the Satyashodhak Samaj, an association that advocated social reforms and challenged Brahmin domination of Maratha political and cultural life. In 1882 she wrote a Marathi treatise on gender relations, 'Stri-Purush Tulana' (A Comparison Between Women and Men), which took a very critical view of the treatment that Indian women were receiving from Indian men; in particular she objected to the increasingly common practice of women being blamed for the ills within Indian society.

Singh, Ranjit (1780–1839) Appointed governor of Lahore by the Afghans in 1798 when they ruled the region, Ranjit Singh managed to weld the disparate communities in the Punjab into a coherent state, equipped with a modernized army, which he would use to gain independence from the Afghans. Under his rule, the Punjab was a stable and prosperous region and through effective diplomacy he was able to keep the British at bay.

Siraj-ad-daula (d.1757) Born sometime between 1729 and 1738, Siraj-ad-daula became Nawab of Bengal on the death of his grandfather, Alivardi Khan, in 1755. Faced with mounting challenges to his authority from the British as well as powerful magnates and *zamindar*s in Bengal, Siraj-ad-daula tried to impose greater controls on all of them. This would, however, backfire as a conspiracy soon developed between the British, discontented bankers and merchants, and ambitious nobles. He died soon after the Battle of Plassey.

Tantia Topi (d.1859) Otherwise known as Ramchandra, son of Panda Rang. A Brahmin from Pune, he had joined Nana Sahib where he proved to be one of the most skilled commanders during the Indian Rebellion. Following the British recapture of Kanpur, he went south to Jhansi where he helped to organize its defence against the British. He resorted to guerilla tactics and eluded the British until April 1859 when he was captured and executed.

Tipu Sultan (d.1799) The son and heir of Haidar Ali, Tipu Sultan continued his father's struggle to maintain the independence of Mysore in the face of British expansion. Yet the odds were increasingly stacked against him, and when he tried for an alliance with France, this gave the British the excuse they needed to bring his reign to an end. He died following the capture of Seringapatam in 1799.

British propagandists turned him into a symbol of Muslim fanaticism though close scrutiny suggests that this image has been overblown.

Wellesley, Richard (1760–1842) Born into the Irish aristocracy, Wellesley entered politics in 1784. He was sent to India as governor-general in 1797 and would return to Britain in 1806. Wellesley was one of the most energetic and ambitious governor-generals sent to India, and dedicated his efforts to ensuring that Britain became the paramount power in India. This brought him into conflict not only with a number of Indian powers, several of which like Mysore were decisively defeated in battle, but also with the East India Company who feared the financial and political consequences of his actions.

CHAPTER ONE

A number of very good surveys of Indian history are currently in print which cover the grand sweep of Indian history. See, for example, Burton Stein, *A History of India* (Malden, Mass.: Blackwell Publishers, 1998). More recently, Claude Markovits has assembled a team of French scholars who have put together one of the most comprehensive histories of India dealing with the period since 1480: Claude Markovits, ed., *A History of Modern India, 1480–1950* (London: Anthem Press, 2002). And John Keay's *India: A History* (New York: Grove, 2000) would be a good choice for anyone wanting a well-written and conventionally ordered narrative of the course of Indian history. For the modern period, two extremely lucid studies which engage with the most recent scholarship are Sugata Bose and Ayesha Jalal, *Modern South Asia: History, Culture, Political Economy* (New York: Routledge, 1998) and Barbara D. Metcalf and Thomas Metcalf, *A Concise History of India* (Cambridge: Cambridge University Press, 2002). Judith M. Brown, *Modern India: The Origins of Asian Democracy*, 2nd edn (Oxford: Oxford University Press, 1994) is very good on detailing the political history of modern India. And for the period after 1885, Sumit Sarkar's *Modern India* (London: Macmillan, 1989) is highly recommended for Sarkar brings the perspectives of a social historian to bear on the history of the nationalist movement in India, and offers a counterbalance to earlier works that interpreted nationalism largely in terms of purely political processes controlled by the elites. Much of the latest research on Indian history can be found, as well as the underlying historiographical debates, in the multi-volumed *New Cambridge History of India*, which has been appearing in instalments since 1988. Single-authored works of high quality, they cover a range of themes in the history of India since 1500 and more will be appearing. Individual titles will be noted later, but one which tackles some of the broad themes addressed here is C.A. Bayly, *Indian Society and the Making of the British Empire: The New Cambridge History of India, II.1* (Cambridge: Cambridge University Press, 1988). Equally useful are the volumes on ideology and the state, Thomas R. Metcalf, *Ideologies of the Raj: The New Cambridge History of India, III.4* (Cambridge: Cambridge University Press, 1994) and Geraldine Forbes's survey of the history of women in modern India, Geraldine H. Forbes, *Women in Modern India: New Cambridge History of India, IV.2* (Cambridge: Cambridge University Press, 1996). The latter should be read in conjunction with Tanika Sarkar's excellent collection of essays in *Hindu Wife, Hindu Nation: Community, Religion and Cultural Nationalism.* (New Delhi: Permanent Black, 2001).

The chapters on India by P.J. Marshall, Huw Bowen, David Washbrook, Rajat Ray, R.J. Moore and Judith M. Brown in the *Oxford History of the British Empire* (1998–99) place modern India within the context of the history of the British Empire, and draw attention to the links between what was happening in the wider empire and developments in India. C.A. Bayly, ed., *The Raj: India and the British, 1600–1947*

(London: National Portrait Gallery, 1990), which was published to accompany a major exhibition in London, cannot be matched for the variety or quality of the visual images it contains and it also provides a number of stimulating essays on such topics as the aesthetics of Britain's encounter with India, colonial ethnography, art and nationalism in India, and the history of photography in India. Volume two of the *Cambridge Economic History of India* provides a wealth of information on the economic transformation of India under colonial rule, though the essays taken together have been accused of downplaying colonialism in favour of an interpretation that stresses continuities rather than change: Dharma Kumar, ed., *The Cambridge Economic History of India*, Vol. 2 (Cambridge: Cambridge University Press, 1983). For a discussion of the state of Indian economic history which is still pertinent today, see David Washbrook, 'Progress and Problems: South Asian Economic and Social History, c.1720–1860', *Modern Asian Studies* 22 (1988): 57–96.

One of the most exciting developments in the history of India has been provided by the subaltern studies collective, a loose coalition of historians and activists who were dissatisfied with the elitist nature of much of the existing scholarship on India, particularly with reference to the origins of Indian nationalism, and who looked to bring in hitherto silenced voices to correct what they saw as a preoccupation with elites. Informed by a range of political and philosophical positions and perspectives, their work has been heavily influenced by social historians such as E.P. Thompson, Marxist political philosophers like Antonio Gramsci and, more recently, by the works of such post-colonial critics as Edward Said and Gayatri Spivak. A very useful compilation of some of their earliest works is Ranajit Guha and Gayatri Chakravorty Spivak, eds, *Selected Subaltern Studies* (Oxford: Oxford University Press, 1988). Ranajit Guha, one of the founders of the collective, offers an important retrospect on their contributions in *Dominance without Hegemony: History and Power in Colonial India* (Cambridge, Mass.: Harvard University Press, 1998). See also his *Elementary Aspects of Peasant Insurgency in Colonial India* (Delhi: Oxford University Press, 1983) for an example of their pioneering work in recovering peasant voices. Another valuable collection of essays on the contributions made by subaltern studies, as well as some critical reflections on their limits, is David Ludden, ed., *Reading Subaltern Studies: Critical History, Contested Meaning, and the Globalization of South Asia* (London: Anthem Press, 2002). One of the early contributors to their publications, Sumit Sarkar, expressed some of the misgivings that he and others have felt with what they saw as a growing preoccupation with postmodernism and a corresponding failure on the part of subaltern studies to take adequate notice of the material forces in history in Sumit Sarkar, *Beyond Nationalist Frames: Postmodernism, Hindu Fundamentalism, History* (Bloomington: Indiana University Press, 2002).

For readers wishing for more information on the historical geography of India, the single best source for maps of India is to be found in Joseph Schwartzberg, *A Historical Atlas of South Asia* (Chicago: University of Chicago Press, 1978). The relationship between geographical knowledge and British power in India is carefully dissected in Matthew H. Edney, *Mapping an Empire: The Geographical Construction of British India, 1765–1843* (Chicago: University of Chicago Press, 1997). The recent interest in the relationship between environment and history can be followed in several fine studies: Madhav Gadgil and Ramachandra Guha, *This Fissured Land: An Ecological History of India* (Berkeley: University of California Press, 1993); Mahesh Rangarajan, *India's Wildlife History: An Introduction* (New Delhi: Permanent Black, 2001), and in the essays to be found in David Arnold and Ramachandra Guha,

Nature, Culture, Imperialism: Essays on the Environmental History of South Asia (Delhi: Oxford University Press, 1995). As a general reference work, Parshotam Mehra, ed., *A Dictionary of Modern Indian History, 1707–1947* (Delhi: Oxford University Press, 1987) is useful.

One of the biggest challenges in seeking to gain a historical understanding of India is to try and make sense of caste. This task has been made more difficult by the realization that caste itself is a moving target, and much of what we think of as caste is in fact a product of colonial rule. An excellent introduction to the subject of caste as well as other Indian social customs and identities can be found in Bernard Cohn, *India: The Social Anthropology of a Civilization*, 2nd edn (New Delhi: Oxford University Press, 2000). The degree to which caste and other allegedly traditional aspects of Indian identity were the product of colonial rule features in a number of studies; some of the more pertinent ones include Ronald Inden, 'Orientalist Constructions of India', *Modern Asian Studies* 20 (1986); Susan Bayly, *Caste, Society and Politics in India from the Eighteenth Century to the Modern Age: The New Cambridge History of India, IV.3* (Cambridge: Cambridge University Press, 1999); and Nicholas Dirks, *Castes of Mind: Colonialism and the Making of Modern India* (Princeton: Princeton University Press, 2001). The issue of how identities like caste and religion came to be defined in the modern period is tied in with broader questions of colonial knowledge. A lively debate has been ongoing for some time on the subject of oriental knowledge and it can be followed through the following titles in addition to those already listed: Bernard S. Cohn, *Colonialism and Its Forms of Knowledge: The British in India.* (Princeton: Princeton University Press, 1996); Carol A. Breckenridge and Peter van der Veer, eds, *Orientalism and the Post-Colonial Predicament: Perspectives on South Asia* (Philadelphia: University of Pennsylvania Press, 1993), and Thomas R. Trautmann, *Aryans and British India* (Berkeley: University of California Press, 1996).

CHAPTER TWO

The single best introduction to the history of the Mughals is John F. Richards, *The Mughal Empire: The New Cambridge History of India, I.5* (Cambridge: Cambridge University Press, 1993). It is particularly strong on the political organization of the Mughals. It can usefully be read in conjunction with Harbans Mukhia's recent work, *The Mughals* (Oxford: Blackwell, 2004), which has more of a cultural and ideological focus. The various essays reprinted in Muzaffar Alam and Sanjay Subrahmanyam, eds, *The Mughal State, 1526–1750* (Delhi: Oxford University Press, 1998) will provide not only further detail on the Mughals but also highlight some of the ongoing debates over their history, including the contentious issue of explaining their demise. Perhaps the most important revisionist account of the Mughals is Muzaffar Alam's *The Crisis of Empire in Mughal North India: Awadh and the Punjab, 1707–1748* (Delhi: Oxford University Press, 1986), which makes a convincing case for rejecting earlier theories of Mughal decline. It can be complemented by Richard B. Barnett's *North India between Empires: Awadh, the Mughals, and the British, 1720–1801* (Berkeley: University of California Press, 1980), which provides a close analysis of the transition from Mughal to British authority in one locale. The emergence of various ethnically or religiously defined alternatives to the Mughals can be traced in Stewart Gordon, *The Marathas, 1600–1818: The New Cambridge History of India, II.4* (Cambridge: Cambridge University Press, 1993) and J.S. Grewal, *The Sikhs of the Punjab: The*

New Cambridge History of India, II.3 (Cambridge: Cambridge University Press, 1991).

The trading world of the Indian Ocean has been the subject of two important works by K.N. Chaudhuri: *Trade and Civilisation in the Indian Ocean: An Economic Analysis from the Rise of Islam to 1750* (Cambridge: Cambridge University Press, 1985) is particularly strong on the economics of the Indian Ocean while his subsequent *Asia before Europe: Economy and Civilisation of the Indian Ocean from the Rise of Islam to 1750* (Cambridge: Cambridge University Press, 1991) attempts with some success to plug the economics into a wider cultural framework (though the first section in which he seeks to employ mathematical set theory to make his case can be disregarded). A comparison of the strategies and activities of the various European powers is provided in Om Prakash, *European Commercial Enterprise in Pre-Colonial India: The New Cambridge History of India, II.5* (Cambridge: Cambridge University Press, 1998). Holden Furber's *Rival Empires of Trade in the Orient, 1600–1800* (Minneapolis: University of Minnesota Press, 1976), while somewhat dated, provides a very readable overview. For the Portuguese in south India, the works of Sanjay Subrahmanyam are an obvious starting point, see, for example, his *The Portuguese Empire in Asia, 1500–1700: A Political and Economic History* (Harlow: Longman, 1992). Also useful is his assessment of the state of historiography for this earlier period, Sanjay Subrahmanyam, 'Introduction: Making Sense of Indian Historiography', *Indian Economic and Social History Review* 39 (2002): 121–30. The relationship between what was happening in the Indian Ocean world and the wider global economy has been provocatively discussed in the contributions to Sugata Bose, ed., *South Asia and World Capitalism* (Delhi: Oxford University Press, 1990). A good one-volume history of the East India Company is Philip Lawson's *The East India Company: A History* (London: Longman, 1993).

The course of events and underlying processes which yielded Bengal to the British are lucidly addressed in P.J. Marshall, *Bengal: The British Bridgehead, Eastern India, 1740–1828* (Cambridge: Cambridge University Press, 1988). Two excellent studies which delve more deeply into the nature of agrarian society in Bengal during the early stages of British rule are Sugata Bose, *Peasant Labour and Colonial Capital: Rural Bengal since 1770: The New Cambridge History of India, III.2* (Cambridge: Cambridge University Press, 1993) and Rajat Datta, *Society, Economy and the Market: Commercialization in Rural Bengal, c.1760–1800* (New Delhi: Manohar, 2000). Other important works that consider the economic and social transformations which occurred during this period, and their relationship to imperial rule, are C.A. Bayly's seminal study of towns and villages on the Gangetic Plain, *Rulers, Townsmen and Bazaars: North Indian Society in the Age of Expansion, 1770–1870* (Cambridge: Cambridge University Press, 1983) and David Ludden's wide-ranging and ambitious study of peasant society, *An Agrarian History of South Asia: The New Cambridge History of India, IV.4* (Cambridge: Cambridge University Press, 1999).

Of late, there has been a noticeable increase in interest in Indians who travelled to Britain, their experiences there as well as the impressions they gained of western society. Two general works that provide an abundance of insights into early Indian encounters with Great Britain are Michael Fisher, *Counterflows to Colonialism: Indian Travelers and Settlers in Britain, 1600–1857* (New Delhi: Permanent Black, 2004); and Rozina Visram, *Asians in Britain: 400 Years of History* (London: Pluto Press, 2002). Michael Fisher's *The First Indian Author in English: Dean Mahomed (1759–1851) in India, Ireland, and England* (Delhi: Oxford University Press, 1996) can also be recommended for it provides a fascinating first-hand account of the often ambivalent position in which such travellers found themselves.

CHAPTER THREE

In addition to several of the works already mentioned on the origins and expansion of British rule in India, notably Bayly's *Indian Society and the Making of the British Empire* and Marshall's *Bengal: The British Bridgehead*, there have been a number of detailed studies of particular strategic priorities that informed British policy-making. The so-called great game is the subject of Edward Ingram's trilogy, *The Beginnings of the Great Game in Asia, 1828–1834* (Oxford: Clarendon Press, 1979); *Commitment to Empire: Prophecies of the Great Game in Asia, 1797–1800* (Oxford: Clarendon Press, 1981); and *Britain's Persian Connection, 1798–1828: Prelude to the Great Game in Asia* (Oxford: Clarendon Press, 1992); and Malcolm Yapp, *Strategies of British India: Britain, Iran and Afghanistan, 1798–1850* (Oxford: Clarendon Press, 1980). The place of the military in not only enabling conquest but also in shaping many of the ideologies and institutions of colonial rule has been studied in several works which roughly fall within what has been termed the new military history: Seema Alavi, *The Sepoys and the Company: Tradition and Transition in Northern India, 1770–1830* (Delhi: Oxford University Press, 1995); Dirk H.A. Kolff, *Naukar, Rajput, and Sepoy: The Ethnohistory of the Military Labour Market of Hindustan, 1450–1850* (Cambridge: Cambridge University Press, 1990); Douglas M. Peers, *Between Mars and Mammon: Colonial Armies and the Garrison State in Early-Nineteenth Century India* (London: Tauris, 1995); and for the later period, David Omissi, *The Sepoy and the Raj: The Indian Army, 1860–1940* (London: Macmillan, 1994). The policies of indirect rule and the histories of native states are the subject of Michael H. Fisher, *Indirect Rule in the British Empire: Residents and the Residency System in India, 1764–1857* (Delhi: Oxford University Press, 1991) and Barbara N. Ramusack, *The Indian Princes and their States: The New Cambridge History of India, III.6* (Cambridge: Cambridge University Press, 2004).

The political debates which ensued in Britain as a consequence of the revolution in Bengal can be followed in P.J. Marshall, *The Impeachment of Warren Hastings* (Oxford: Oxford University Press, 1965), and in H.V. Bowen, *Revenue and Reform: The Indian Problem in British Politics, 1757–1773* (Cambridge: Cambridge University Press, 1991). Questions of ideology and information, and how they shaped colonial rule in India are covered in C.A. Bayly, *Empire and Information: Intelligence Gathering and Social Communication in India, 1780–1870* (Cambridge: Cambridge University Press, 1996), and Metcalf's *Ideologies of the Raj* to which reference has already been made. The classic liberal interpretation of British intentions in India can be seen in G.D. Bearce, *British Attitudes Towards India, 1784–1858* (Oxford: Oxford University Press, 1961) as well as in David Kopf's *British Orientalism and the Bengal Renaissance: The Dynamics of Indian Modernization, 1773–1835* (Berkeley: University of California Press, 1969). More critical perspectives on the relationship between liberalism and imperialism can be found in Lynn Zastoupil, *John Stuart Mill and India* (Stanford: Stanford University Press, 1994); John Rosselli, *Lord William Bentinck: The Making of a Liberal Imperialist, 1774–1839* (Berkeley: University of California Press, 1974); and Uday Singh Mehta, *Liberalism and Empire: A Study in Nineteenth Century British Liberal Thought* (Chicago: University of Chicago Press,

2000). The role of missionaries in colonial India is the topic of Jeffrey Cox's finely-balanced and nuanced study, *Imperial Fault Lines: Christianity and Colonial Power in India, 1818–1940* (Stanford: Stanford University Press, 2002), which can be usefully read in conjunction with A.N. Porter's *Religion Versus Empire? British Protestant Missionaries and Overseas Expansion, 1700–1914* (Manchester: Manchester University Press, 2004) that will help to place what was happening in India within a wider imperial context.

The place of science and medicine in colonial India is a critical and fascinating topic though one which could not be adequately addressed in this book. Readers interested in such questions should look at David Arnold, *Science, Technology and Medicine in Colonial India: The New Cambridge History of India, III:5* (Cambridge: Cambridge University Press, 2000); Richard H. Grove, *Green Imperialism: Colonial Expansion, Tropical Island Edens and the Origins of Environmentalism, 1600–1860* (Cambridge: Cambridge University Press, 1995); Mark Harrison, *Climates and Constitutions: Health, Race, Environment and British Imperialism in India* (Delhi: Oxford University Press, 1999); and Deepak Kumar, *Science and the Raj* (Delhi: Oxford University Press, 1995).

British efforts to enhance and systematize the collection of revenues, and their consequences, are explored in Bose, *Peasant Labour and Colonial Capital* and Ludden, *Agrarian History of South Asia*, of which mention has already been made. The intellectual roots of the permanent settlement are explored in Ranajit Guha, *A Rule of Property for Bengal: An Essay on the Idea of the Permanent Settlement* (Durham, N.C.: Duke University Press, 1995). For the *ryotwari* system in use in southern India, see Burton Stein, *Thomas Munro: The Origins of the Colonial State and his Vision of Empire* (Delhi: Oxford University Press, 1989) as well as the essays in Burton Stein, ed., *The Making of Agrarian Policy in British India, 1770–1900* (Delhi: Oxford University Press, 1992). Western India is covered in Sumit Guha's *The Agrarian Economy of the Bombay Deccan, 1818–1941* (Delhi: Oxford University Press, 1985). The role of law in sustaining colonial authority has been tackled in Radhika Singha's detailed and judicious study, *A Despotism of Law: Crime and Justice in Early Colonial India* (Delhi: Oxford University Press, 1998), and the essays in Anand A. Yang, ed., *Crime and Criminality in British India* (Tucson: University of Arizona Press, 1985) provide several fascinating examples of how law functioned in practice. By far the best work on *sati* is Lata Mani's *Contentious Traditions: The Debate on Sati in Colonial India* (Berkeley: University of California Press, 1998) and Martine Van Woerkens, *The Strangled Traveler: Colonial Imaginings and the Thugs of India*, translated by Catherine Tihanyi (Chicago: University of Chicago Press, 2002) is a very original if sometimes opaque study of the reality as well as the imagined world of the thugs.

CHAPTER FOUR

The Indian Rebellion has been the subject of countless books and articles, but alas many of them do little more than provide exhaustive and exhausting accounts of military campaigns and/or reinforce dated stereotypes about the rebels. There are, however, some notable exceptions. Saul David has recently published a bracing if somewhat conventional narrative of the military history of the rebellion, *The Indian Mutiny, 1857* (London: Viking, 2002). Facts galore can be found in P.J.O. Taylor,

A Companion to the 'Indian Mutiny' of 1857 (Delhi: Oxford University Press, 1996) and *What Really Happened During the Mutiny: A Day-by-Day Account of the Major Events of 1857–1859 in India* (Delhi: Oxford University Press, 1997). Eric Stokes, *The Peasant Armed* (Oxford: Oxford University Press, 1986) consists of a series of loosely connected essays which consider, among other things, the military dimensions to the revolt and reasons for peasant participation, with an emphasis on the differences as much as the similarities among the rebels. An alternative perspective is provided in Rudrangshu Mukherjee, *Awadh in Revolt, 1857–1858: A Study in Popular Resistance* (Delhi: Oxford University Press, 1984) wherein a case is made for treating the rebellion as a genuine popular movement, although not quite a war of independence. Tapti Roy, *The Politics of a Popular Uprising: Bundelkhand in 1857* (Delhi: Oxford University Press, 1994) is a detailed and scholarly account of the rebellion in a particular locale.

The post-rebellion settlement is the subject of Thomas R. Metcalf, *Aftermath of Revolt: India, 1857–1870* (Princeton: Princeton University Press, 1964). The economic changes which India experienced, and the degree to which colonial rule can be held accountable, are the focus of two recent surveys of modern Indian economic history: B.R. Tomlinson, *The Economy of Modern India, 1860–1970: The New Cambridge History of India, III.3* (Cambridge: Cambridge University Press, 1993) and Tirthankar Roy, *The Economic History of India, 1857–1947* (New Delhi: Oxford University Press, 2000). The latter has proved to be rather controversial on account of its rejection of the nationalist arguments about colonialism being a drain on the Indian economy. The question of how imperial policies affected the textile industry is addressed in Peter Harnetty, '"Deindustrialisation" Revisited: The Handloom Weavers of the Central Provinces of India, c.1800–1947', *Modern Asian Studies* 25 (3) (1991): 455–510. One of the more contentious issues in modern Indian history is the extent to which colonial rule can be held accountable for the devastation and loss of life occasioned by famines in India. A good introduction to these debates is offered in David Arnold, *Famine: Social Crisis and Historical Change* (Oxford: Blackwell, 1988), with more specialized treatment appearing in M.B. McAlpin, *Subject to Famine: Food Crises and Economic Change in Western India, 1860–1920* (Princeton: Princeton University Press, 1983). The history of indentured labour is surveyed in David Northrup, *Indentured Labor in the Age of Imperialism, 1834–1922* (Cambridge: Cambridge University Press, 1995).

The more intrusive character of post-1857 colonial rule was manifested in a number of ways: censuses, codification of criminal law, and sanitary and medical policies. In addition to the aforementioned works by S. Bayly on caste, and Bernard Cohn and Chris Bayly on colonial knowledge, there are a number of valuable case studies. On the census, see Sumit Guha, 'The Politics of Identity and Enumeration in India, c.1600–1900', *Comparative Studies in Society and History* 45(1) (2003): 148–67. The relationship between western medicine and colonial authority is the subject of David Arnold, *Colonizing the Body: State Medicine and Epidemic Disease in Nineteenth-Century India* (Berkeley: University of California Press, 1993), while Philippa Levine's *Prostitution, Race and Politics: Policing Venereal Disease in the British Empire* (London: Routledge, 2003) provides an absorbing account of British efforts to curb venereal disease within the ranks of their troops in India as well as elsewhere in the British Empire.

A good deal has been written on the subject of religious revival and reform in late nineteenth-century India. For a summary account of many of the resulting movements like Arya Samaj, see Kenneth W. Jones, *Socio-Religious Movements in British India: The New Cambridge History of India, III.1* (Cambridge: Cambridge University Press, 1989). A more critical perspective, and one which places the onus for the intensified communal antagonisms in India on the impact of colonial policies and the workings of colonial knowledge systems, can be found in Gyanendra Pandey, *The Construction of Communalism in Colonial North India* (Delhi: Oxford University Press, 1990). Mushirul Hasan's *A Moral Reckoning: Muslim Intellectuals in Nineteenth-Century Delhi* (Delhi: Oxford University Press, 2005) is a recent study of how a select group of Muslims in Delhi responded to the changes happening around them. The emergence of a more vigorous public sphere in which greater debate and discussion over religious and cultural questions could occur is the subject of Sandria B. Freitag, *Collective Action and Community: Public Arenas and the Emergence of Communalism in North India* (Berkeley: University of California Press, 1989). Tapati Guha Thakurta, *The Making of the New 'Indian' Art: Artists, Aesthetics and Nationalism in Bengal, c.1850–1920* (Cambridge: Cambridge University Press, 1992) and Partha Mitter, *Art and Nationalism in Colonial India, 1850–1922: Occidental Orientations* (Cambridge: Cambridge University Press, 1995) look at how Indian art and aesthetics responded to colonial rule, while Priya Joshi in *In Another Country: British Popular Fiction and the Development of the English Novel in India* (New York: Columbia University Press, 2002) examines the relationship between British literary culture and the growing popularity of the novel in nineteenth-century India. The manner in which imperial values and ethos were inscribed in architecture is the subject of Thomas R. Metcalf, *An Imperial Vision: Indian Architecture and Britain's Raj* (Berkeley: University of California Press, 1989).

A number of the most provocative and original studies of nineteenth-century India have taken questions of gender as their point of departure. In addition to the works of Geraldine Forbes and Tanika Sarkar already mentioned, see the various essays in Kumkum Sangari, ed., *Recasting Women: Essays in Indian Colonial History* (New Jersey: Rutgers University Press, 1990), and J. Krishnamurty, ed., *Women in Colonial India: Essays on Survival, Work and the State* (Delhi: Oxford University Press, 1989). Rosalind O'Hanlon, *A Comparison between Women and Men: Tarabai Shinde and the Critique of Gender Relations in Colonial India* (Madras: Oxford University Press, 1994) not only provides a translation of Tarabai Shinde's critique of how women were then treated but accompanies it with a lengthy essay that sets out very effectively the context for Shinde's writing. Another influential early Indian feminist and writer, Pandita Ramabai is the subject of another excellent translation: *Pandita Ramabai's American Encounter: The Peoples of the United States (1889)*, translated by Meera Kosambi (Bloomington: Indiana University Press, 2003). Once again readers will find not only valuable insights into the mental world of the nineteenth century but can learn much from Kosambi's introduction and footnotes to the text. How Indian feminists were received by and responded to Victorian society is the subject of Antoinette Burton's *At the Heart of Empire: Indians and the Colonial Encounter in Late-Victorian Britain* (Berkeley: University of California Press, 1997) which followed on from her pathbreaking book on British feminists and India, *Burdens of History: British Feminists, Indian Women, and Imperial Culture, 1865–1915* (Chapel Hill, N.C.: University of North Carolina Press, 1994). Also recommended is Mrinalini Sinha, *Colonial Masculinity: The 'Englishman' and the 'Effeminate Bengali' in the Late Nineteenth Century* (Manchester: Manchester

University Press, 1995), which considers the reasons for and the consequences of the growing preoccupation with masculinity in colonial India.

One of the classic accounts of the rise of nationalism is Anil Seal, *The Emergence of Indian Nationalism: Competition and Collaboration in the Later Nineteenth Century* (Cambridge: Cambridge University Press, 1968), a work which has proved to be very controversial on account of its emphasis on elites and self-interest as the driving force behind nationalism. Sumit Sarkar's *Modern India* as previously mentioned offers a different and for many a more acceptable way of approaching the beginnings of nationalism. An even more radical line of argument is advanced in Partha Chatterjee, *The Nation and Its Fragments: Colonial and Postcolonial Histories* (Princeton: Princeton University Press, 1993). Peter van der Veer, *Religious Nationalism: Hindus and Muslims in India* (Berkeley: University of California Press, 1994) is a useful introduction for anyone wishing to look more closely at how religion and nationalism were becoming enmeshed in the late nineteenth and twentieth centuries.

REFERENCES

Alam, M. (1986) *The Crisis of Empire in Mughal North India: Awadh and the Punjab, 1707–1748*. Delhi, Oxford University Press.

Alavi, S. (1995) *The Sepoys and the Company: Tradition and Transition in Northern India, 1770–1830*. Delhi, Oxford University Press.

Arnold, D. (1986) *Police Power and Colonial Rule: Madras, 1859–1947*. Delhi, Oxford University Press.

Baird, J.G., ed. (1910) *Private Letters of the Marquess of Dalhousie*. Edinburgh, Blackwood.

Barnett, R.B. (1980) *North India between Empires: Awadh, the Mughals, and the British, 1720–1801*. Berkeley, University of California Press.

Bayly, C.A. (1983) *Rulers, Townsmen and Bazaars: North Indian Society in the Age of Expansion, 1770–1870*. Cambridge, Cambridge University Press.

Bayly, C.A. (1988) *Indian Society and the Making of the British Empire: The New Cambridge History of India, II.1*. Cambridge, Cambridge University Press.

Bayly, C.A. (1996) *Empire and Information: Intelligence Gathering and Social Communication in India, 1780–1870*. Cambridge, Cambridge University Press.

Bayly, S. (1999) *Caste, Society and Politics in India from the Eighteenth Century to the Modern Age: The New Cambridge History of India, IV.3*. Cambridge, Cambridge University Press.

Bearce, G.D. (1961) *British Attitudes towards India, 1784–1858*. Oxford, Oxford University Press.

Bose, S., ed. (1990) *South Asia and World Capitalism*. Delhi, Oxford University Press.

Bose, S. (1993) *Peasant Labour and Colonial Capital: Rural Bengal since 1770: The New Cambridge History of India, III.2*. Cambridge, Cambridge University Press.

Bose, S. and A. Jalal, eds (1998) *Modern South Asia: History, Culture, Political Economy*. New York, Routledge.

Bowen, H. (1998) British India, 1765–1813: The Metropolitan Context. *The Oxford History of the British Empire: The Eighteenth Century*, P.J. Marshall. Oxford, Oxford University Press.

Bowen, H.V. (1991) *Revenue and Reform: The Indian Problem in British Politics, 1757–1773*. Cambridge, Cambridge University Press.

Burton, A. (1994) *Burdens of History: British Feminists, Indian Women, and Imperial Culture, 1865–1915*. Chapel Hill, N.C., University of North Carolina Press.

Chatterji, Bankimcandra (2005) *Anandamath, or The Sacred Brotherhood*, translated by Julius Lipner. Oxford, Oxford University Press.

Chaudhuri, K.N. (1985) *Trade and Civilisation in the Indian Ocean: An Economic Analysis from the Rise of Islam to 1750*. Cambridge, Cambridge University Press.

Chaudhuri, K.N. (1991) *Asia before Europe: Economy and Civilisation of the Indian Ocean from the Rise of Islam to 1750*. Cambridge, Cambridge University Press.

Chaudhury, S. (1995) *From Prosperity to Decline: Eighteenth-Century Bengal*. Delhi, Manohar.

Chaudhury, S. (2001) 'English Takes India from Raj to Riches', *Times Higher Education Supplement*: 20–1.

Cohn, B.S. (1996) *Colonialism and its Forms of Knowledge: The British in India*. Princeton, Princeton University Press.

Colley, L. (2002) *Captives: Britain, Empire and the World, 1600–1850*. London, Cape.

Collingham, Lizzie (2005) *Curry: A Biography*. London, Chatto & Windus.

Cooper, R.G.S. (2003) *The Anglo-Maratha Campaigns and the Contest for India: The Struggle for Control of the South Asian Military Economy*. Cambridge, Cambridge University Press.

Cox, J. (2002) *Imperial Fault Lines: Christianity and Colonial Power in India, 1818–1940*. Stanford, Stanford University Press.

Dalrymple, W. (2002) *White Mughals: Love and Betrayal in Eighteenth-Century India*. London, HarperCollins.

Datta, R. (2000) *Society, Economy and the Market: Commercialization in Rural Bengal, c.1760–1800*. New Delhi, Manohar.

David, S. (2002) *The Indian Mutiny, 1857*. London, Viking.

Davis, M. (2000) *Late Victorian Holocausts: El Nino Famines and the Making of the Third World*. London, Verso.

Dirks, N. (2001) *Castes of Mind: Colonialism and the Making of Modern India*. Princeton, Princeton University Press.

Downs, T. (2002) 'Rajput Dakaiti and Bhumeawati in Janupur: The Careers of Dakait Leader Sangram Singh, 1857–1867', *South Asia* 25(1): 21–47.

Drayton, R. (2000) *Nature's Government: Science, British Imperialism and the 'Improvement' of the World*. New Haven, Yale University Press.

Farnie, D.A. (1979) *The English Cotton Industry and the World Market, 1815–1896*. Oxford, Oxford University Press.

Fisher, M. (1996) *The First Indian Author in English: Dean Mahomed (1759–1851) in India, Ireland, and England*. Delhi, Oxford University Press.

Fisher, M. (2004) *Counterflows to Colonialism: Indian Travelers and Settlers in Britain, 1600–1857*. New Delhi, Permanent Black.

Forbes, G.H. (1996) *Women in Modern India: New Cambridge History of India, IV.2*. Cambridge, Cambridge University Press.

Franklin, M.J. (1995) *Sir William Jones*. Cardiff, University of Wales Press.

Freitag, S.B. (1989) *Collective Action and Community: Public Arenas and the Emergence of Communalism in North India*. Berkeley, University of California Press.

Furber, H. (1976) *Rival Empires of Trade in the Orient, 1600–1800*. Minneapolis, University of Minnesota Press.

Gadgil, M. and R. Guha (1993) *This Fissured Land: An Ecological History of India*. Berkeley, University of California Press.

Ghosh, D. (2004) 'Household Crimes and Domestic Order: Keeping the Peace in Colonial Calcutta, c.1770–c.1840', *Modern Asian Studies* 38(3): 599–623.

Gilmartin, D. (1994) 'Scientific Empire and Imperial Science: Colonialism and Irrigation Technology in the Indus Basin', *Journal of Asian Studies* 53: 1127–49.

Gommans, J. (2002) *Mughal Warfare: Indian Frontiers and High Roads to Empire, 1500–1700*. London, Routledge.

Gordon, S. (1993) *The Marathas, 1600–1818: The New Cambridge History of India, II.4*. Cambridge, Cambridge University Press.

Gordon, S. (1998) 'The Limited Adoption of European Style Military Forces by Eighteenth-Century Rulers in India', *Indian Economic and Social History Review* 35(3): 229–45.

Greenberg, M. (1969) *British Trade and the Opening of China, 1800–1842.* Cambridge, Cambridge University Press.

Grewal, J.S. (1991) *The Sikhs of the Punjab: The New Cambridge History of India, II.3.* Cambridge, Cambridge University Press.

Guha, R. (1983) *Elementary Aspects of Peasant Insurgency in Colonial India.* Delhi, Oxford University Press.

Guha, R. (1990) *The Unquiet Woods: Ecological Change and Peasant Resistance in the Himalaya.* Berkeley, University of California Press.

Guha, R. (1995) *A Rule of Property for Bengal: An Essay on the Idea of the Permanent Settlement.* Durham, N.C., Duke University Press.

Guha, S. (1999) *Environment and Ethnicity in India, 1200–1991.* Cambridge, Cambridge University Press.

Habib, I., ed. (1999) *Confronting Colonialism: Resistance and Modernization under Haidar Ali and Tipu Sultan.* Delhi, Tulika.

Hamilton, W. (1828) *East-India Gazetteer; containing Particular Descriptions of the Empires, Kingdoms, Principalities, etc. of Hindostan.* London.

Hardiman, D., ed. (1992) *Peasant Resistance in India, 1858–1914.* Delhi, Oxford University Press.

Harnetty, P. (1991) ' "Deindustrialisation" Revisited: The Handloom Weavers of the Central Provinces of India, c.1800–1947', *Modern Asian Studies* 25(3): 455–510.

Harrison, M. (1999) *Climates and Constitutions: Health, Race, Environment and British Imperialism in India.* Delhi, Oxford University Press.

Hasan, M. (2005) *A Moral Reckoning: Muslim Intellectuals in Nineteenth-Century Delhi.* Delhi, Oxford University Press.

Hill, S.C. (1914) *Yusuf Khan; the Rebel Commandant.* London, Longmans Green.

Inden, R. (1986) 'Orientalist Constructions of India', *Modern Asian Studies* 20(3): 401–46.

Ingram, E. (1970) *Two views of British India: The Private Correspondence of Mr Dundas and Lord Wellesley, 1798–1801.* Bath, Adams & Dart.

Ingram, E. (1992) *Britain's Persian Connection, 1798–1828: Prelude to the Great Game in Asia.* Oxford, Clarendon Press.

Ingram, E. (2001) *The British Empire as a World Power.* London, Frank Cass.

Jones, K.W. (1989) *Socio-Religious Movements in British India: The New Cambridge History of India, III.1.* Cambridge, Cambridge University Press.

Joshi, S. (2002) *Fractured Modernity: Making of a Middle Class in Colonial North India.* New Delhi, Oxford University Press.

Kaye, J.W. (1852) 'How We Talked about the Burmese War', *Bentley's Miscellany* 32: 461–70.

Kaye, J.W. and G.B. Malleson (1891) *The Indian Mutiny of 1857*, 4th edn. London, W.H. Allen.

Kejariwal, O.P. (1988) *The Asiatic Society of Bengal and the Discovery of India's Past.* Delhi, Oxford University Press.

Kennedy, D. (1996) 'Imperial History and Post-Colonial Theory', *Journal of Imperial and Commonwealth History* 24: 345–63.

Kerr, I.J. (1995) *Building the Railways of the Raj.* Delhi, Oxford University Press.

Khuhro, H. (2000) *The Making of Modern Sindh: British Policy and Social Change in the Nineteenth Century*. Karachi, Oxford University Press.

Klein, I. (2000) 'Materialism, Mutiny and Modernization in British India', *Modern Asian Studies* 34(3): 545–80.

Kling, B.B. (1966) *The Blue Mutiny: The Indigo Disturbances in Bengal, 1859–1862*. Philadelphia, University of Pennsylvania Press.

Kochanski, H. (2000) *Sir Garnet Wolseley: Victorian Hero*. London, Hambledon.

Kolff, D.H.A. (1990) *Naukar, Rajput, and Sepoy: The Ethnohistory of the Military Labour Market of Hindustan, 1450–1850*. Cambridge, Cambridge University Press.

Kopf, D. (1969) *British Orientalism and the Bengal Renaissance: The Dynamics of Indian Modernization, 1773–1835*. Berkeley, University of California Press.

Kumar, D., ed. (1983) *The Cambridge Economic History of India*. Cambridge, Cambridge University Press.

Lawson, P. (1993) *The East India Company: A History*. London, Longman.

Lelyveld, D. (1996) *Aligarh's First Generation: Muslim Solidarity in British India*. Delhi, Oxford University Press.

Lenman, B. (2000) *Britain's Colonial Wars: 1688–1783*. Harlow, Longman.

Macrory, P.A. (1986) *Kabul Catastrophe: The Story of the Disastrous Retreat from Kabul, 1842*. Oxford, Oxford University Press.

Major, A.J. (1996) *Return to Empire: Punjab under the Sikhs and British in the Mid-nineteenth Century*. New Delhi, Sterling Publishers.

Malcolm, T. (1891) *Barracks and Battlefields in India; or, the Experiences of a Soldier of the 10th Foot (North Lincoln) in the Sikh Wars and Indian Mutiny*. York, John Sampson.

Mani, L. (1998) *Contentious Traditions: The Debate on Sati in Colonial India*. Berkeley, University of California Press.

Marshall, P.J. (1965) *The Impeachment of Warren Hastings*. Oxford, Oxford University Press.

Marshall, P.J. (1976) *East Indian Fortunes: The British in Bengal in the Eighteenth Century*. Oxford, Clarendon Press.

Marshall, P.J. (1988) *Bengal: The British Bridgehead, Eastern India, 1740–1828*. Cambridge, Cambridge University Press.

Marshall, P.J. (1998) The British in Asia: Trade to Dominion, 1700–1765. *The Oxford History of the British Empire: The Eighteenth Century*, P.J. Marshall. Oxford, Oxford University Press.

Marshall, P.J. (2000) 'The White Town of Calcutta under the Rule of the East India Company', *Modern Asian Studies* 43(2): 307–32.

Marshall, P.J., ed. (2003) *The Eighteenth Century in Indian History: Evolution or Revolution?* New Delhi, Oxford University Press.

Mehta, U.S. (2000) *Liberalism and Empire: A Study in Nineteenth-Century British Liberal Thought*. Chicago, University of Chicago Press.

Metcalf, B.D. (1982) *Islamic Revival in British India: Deoband, 1860–1900*. Princeton, Princeton University Press.

Metcalf, B.D. and T. Metcalf (2002) *A Concise History of India*. Cambridge, Cambridge University Press.

Metcalf, T.R. (1964) *Aftermath of Revolt: India, 1857–1870*. Princeton, Princeton University Press.

Metcalf, T.R. (1989) *An Imperial Vision: Indian Architecture and Britain's Raj*. Berkeley, University of California Press.

Metcalf, T.R. (1994) *Ideologies of the Raj: The New Cambridge History of India, III.4.* Cambridge, Cambridge University Press.

Misra, M. (1999) *Business, Race and Politics in British India, c.1850–1960.* Delhi, Oxford University Press.

Mitter, P. (1997) 'Cartoons of the Raj', *History Today* 47: 16–21.

Moore, R.J. (1966) *Sir Charles Wood's Indian Policy, 1853–1866.* Manchester, Manchester University Press.

Mukherjee, R. (1982) 'Trade and Empire in Awadh, 1756–1804', *Past and Present* (94): 85–102.

Mukherjee, R. (1984) *Awadh in Revolt, 1857–1858: A Study in Popular Resistance.* Delhi, Oxford University Press.

Mukherjee, R. (1990) ' "Satan Let Loose upon Earth": The Kanpur Massacres in India in the Revolt of 1857', *Past and Present* (128): 92–116.

Mukhia, H. (2004) *The Mughals.* Oxford, Blackwell.

Nigam, S. (1990) 'Disciplining and Policing the "Criminals by Birth", Part 1: The Making of a Colonial Stereotype – The Criminal Tribes and Castes of North India', *Indian Economic and Social History Review* 27: 131–62.

Northrup, D. (1999) Migration from Africa, Asia, and the South Pacific. *The Oxford History of the British Empire: the Nineteenth Century,* A. Porter. Oxford, Oxford University Press.

Omissi, D. (1994) *The Sepoy and the Raj: The Indian Army, 1860–1940.* London, Macmillan.

Pandey, G. (1990) *The Construction of Communalism in Colonial North India.* Delhi, Oxford University Press.

Panikkar, K.N. (1988) *Against Lord and State: Religion and Peasant Uprisings in Malabar (1836–1921).* Delhi, Oxford University Press.

Paxton, N.L. (1998) *Writing under the Raj: Gender, Race, and Rape in the British Colonial Imagination, 1830–1947.* New Brunswick, N.J., Rutgers University Press.

Peabody, N. (2002) *Hindu Kingship and Polity in Precolonial India.* Cambridge, Cambridge University Press.

Peers, D.M. (1991) 'Torture, the Police and the Colonial State in Madras Presidency, 1816–1855', *Criminal Justice History* 12: 29–56.

Peers, D.M. (1995) *Between Mars and Mammon: Colonial Armies and the Garrison State in Early-Nineteenth Century India.* London, Tauris.

Peers, D.M. (1998) 'Privates Off Parade: Regimenting Sexuality in the Nineteenth Century Indian Empire', *International History Review* 20(4): 823–54.

Peers, D.M. (2003) South Asia. *War in the Modern World since 1815,* J. Black. London, Routledge: 41–74.

Peers, D.M. (2005) 'Colonial Knowledge and the Military in India, 1780–1860', *Journal of Imperial and Commonwealth History* 33(2): 157–80.

Porter, A.N. (2004) *Religion Versus Empire? British Protestant Missionaries and Overseas Expansion, 1700–1914.* Manchester, Manchester University Press.

Prakash, O. (1998) *European Commercial Enterprise in Pre-Colonial India: The New Cambridge History of India, II.5.* Cambridge, Cambridge University Press.

Price, J.M. (1998) The Imperial Economy, 1700–1776. *The Oxford History of the British Empire: The Eighteenth Century,* P.J. Marshall. Oxford, Oxford University Press: 78–104.

Ramusack, B.N. (2004) *The Indian Princes and their States: The New Cambridge History of India, III.6.* Cambridge, Cambridge University Press.

Rangarajan, M. (1994) 'Imperial Agendas and India's Forests: The Early History of Indian Forestry, 1800–1878', *Indian Economic and Social History Review* 31: 147–67.

Ray, R.K. (1998) Indian Society and the Establishment of British Supremacy, 1765–1818. *The Oxford History of the British Empire: The Eighteenth Century*, P.J. Marshall. Oxford, Oxford University Press: 508–29.

Ray, R.K. (2002) *The Felt Community: Commonality and Mentality before the Emergence of Indian Nationalism*. New Delhi, Oxford University Press.

Richards, J.F. (1993) *The Mughal Empire. The New Cambridge History of India, I.5*. Cambridge, Cambridge University Press.

Robinson, F. (2000) *Islam and Muslim History in South Asia*. Delhi, Oxford University Press.

Roy, T. (2000) *The Economic History of India, 1857–1947*. New Delhi, Oxford University Press.

Said, E. (1978) *Orientalism*. London, Routledge.

Sarkar, T. (2001) *Hindu Wife, Hindu Nation: Community, Religion and Cultural Nationalism*. New Delhi, Permanent Black.

Scammell, G.V. (1996) 'European Seafaring in Asia, c.1500–1750', *South Asia* 18: 27–40.

Scott, J.C. (1985) *Weapons of the Weak: Everyday Forms of Peasant Resistance*. New Haven, Yale University Press.

Sen, S.P. (1947) *The French in India: First Establishment and Struggle*. Calcutta, University of Calcutta.

Singha, R. (1998) *A Despotism of Law: Crime and Justice in Early Colonial India*. Delhi, Oxford University Press.

Sinha, M. (1995) *Colonial Masculinity: The 'Englishman' and the 'Effeminate Bengali' in the Late Nineteenth Century*. Manchester, Manchester University Press.

Skaria, A. (1999) *Hybrid Histories: Forests, Frontiers and Wilderness in Western India*. Delhi, Oxford University Press.

Stein, B. (1989) *Thomas Munro: The Origins of the Colonial State and his Vision of Empire*. Delhi, Oxford University Press.

Stein, B., ed. (1992) *The Making of Agrarian Policy in British India, 1700–1900*. Delhi, Oxford University Press.

Stephen, J.F. (1883) 'Foundations of the Government of India', *Nineteenth Century* 80: 541–68.

Stokes, E. (1978) *The Peasant and the Raj*. Cambridge, Cambridge University Press.

Stokes, E. (1986) *The Peasant Armed*. Oxford, Oxford University Press.

Strobel, M. (1991) *European Women and the Second British Empire*. Bloomington, Indiana University Press.

Subrahmanyam, S. (1992) *The Portuguese Empire in Asia, 1500–1700: A Political and Economic History*. Harlow, Longman.

Sutherland, L.S. (1952) *The East India Company in Eighteenth-Century Politics*. Oxford, Clarendon Press.

Tinker, H. (1974) *'A New System of Slavery': The Export of Indian Indentured Labour Overseas, 1830–1920*. Oxford, Oxford University Press.

Tomlinson, B.R. (1993) *The Economy of Modern India, 1860–1970: The New Cambridge History of India, III.3*. Cambridge, Cambridge University Press.

Tomlinson, B.R. (1999) Economics and Empire: The Periphery and the Imperial Economy. *The Oxford History of the British Empire: The Nineteenth Century*, A. Porter. Oxford, Oxford University Press.

Trevithick, A. (1990) 'Some Structural and Sequential Aspects of the British Imperial Assemblages at Delhi, 1877–1911', *Modern Asian Studies* 24: 561–78.

Visram, R. (2002) *Asians in Britain: 400 Years of History*. London, Pluto Press.

Washbrook, D. (1981) 'Law, State and Agrarian Society in Colonial India', *Modern Asian Studies* 15: 649–721.

Washbrook, D. (1999) India, 1818–1860: The Two Faces of Colonialism. *The Oxford History of the British Empire: The Nineteenth Century*, A. Porter. Oxford, Oxford University Press.

Whitcombe, E. (1995) The Environmental Costs of Irrigation in British India: Waterlogging, Salinity and Malaria. *Nature, Culture, Imperialism: Essays on the Environmental History of South Asia*, D. Arnold and R. Guha. New Delhi, Oxford University Press.

Woerkens, M. Van (2002) *The Strangled Traveler: Colonial Imaginings and the Thugs of India*, translated by Catherine Tihanyi. Chicago, University of Chicago Press.

Wong, J.Y. (1998) *Deadly Dreams: Opium and the 'Arrow' War (1856–1860) in China*. Cambridge, Cambridge University Press.

Woodfield, I. (2002) *Music of the Raj: A Social and Economic History of Music in Late Eighteenth-Century Anglo-Indian Society*. New Delhi, Oxford University Press.

Yapp, M. (1980) *Strategies of British India: Britain, Iran and Afghanistan, 1798–1850*. Oxford, Clarendon Press.

Zastoupil, L. and M. Moir, eds (1999) *The Great Indian Education Debate: Documents Relating to the Orientalist-Anglicist Controversy of 1780–1840*. London, Curzon.

INDEX

STUART BRITAIN

Social Change and Continuity: England 1550–1750 (Second edition)
Barry Coward

James I (Second edition)
S. J. Houston

The English Civil War 1640–1649
Martyn Bennett

Charles I, 1625–1640
Brian Quintrell

The English Republic 1649–1660 (Second edition)
Toby Barnard

Radical Puritans in England 1550–1660
R. J. Acheson

The Restoration and the England of Charles II (Second edition)
John Miller

The Glorious Revolution (Second edition)
John Miller

EARLY MODERN EUROPE

The Renaissance (Second edition)
Alison Brown

The Emperor Charles V
Martyn Rady

French Renaissance Monarchy: Francis I and Henry II (Second edition)
Robert Knecht

The Protestant Reformation in Europe
Andrew Johnston

The French Wars of Religion 1559–1598 (Second edition)
Robert Knecht

Phillip II
Geoffrey Woodward

The Thirty Years' War
Peter Limm

Louis XIV
Peter Campbell

Spain in the Seventeenth Century
Graham Darby

Peter the Great
William Marshall

The Origins of French Absolutism, 1598–1661
Alan James

EUROPE 1789–1918

Britain and the French Revolution
Clive Emsley

Revolution and Terror in France 1789–1795 (Second edition)
D. G. Wright

Napoleon and Europe
D. G. Wright

The Abolition of Serfdom in Russia 1762–1907
David Moon

Nineteenth-Century Russia: Opposition to Autocracy
Derek Offord

The Constitutional Monarchy in France 1814–48
Pamela Pilbeam

The 1848 Revolutions (Second edition)
Peter Jones

The Italian Risorgimento
M. Clark

Bismarck & Germany 1862–1890 (Second edition)
D. G. Williamson

Imperial Germany 1890–1918
Ian Porter, Ian Armour and Roger Lockyer

The Dissolution of the Austro-Hungarian Empire 1867–1918 (Second edition)
John W. Mason

Second Empire and Commune: France 1848–1871 (Second edition)
William H. C. Smith

France 1870–1914 (Second edition)
Robert Gildea

The Scramble for Africa (Second edition)
M. E. Chamberlain

Late Imperial Russia 1890–1917
John F. Hutchinson

The First World War
Stuart Robson

Austria, Prussia and Germany 1806–1871
John Breuilly

Napoleon: Conquest, Reform and Reorganisation
Clive Emsley

The French Revolution 1787–1804
Peter Jones

The Origins of the First World War (Third edition)
Gordon Martel

The Birth of Industrial Britain
Kenneth Morgan

EUROPE SINCE 1918

The Russian Revolution (Second edition)
Anthony Wood

Lenin's Revolution: Russia 1917–1921
David Marples

Stalin and Stalinism (Third edition)
Martin McCauley

The Weimar Republic (Second edition)
John Hiden

The Inter-War Crisis 1919–1939
Richard Overy

Fascism and the Right in Europe 1919–1945
Martin Blinkhorn

Spain's Civil War (Second edition)
Harry Browne

The Third Reich (Third edition)
D. G. Williamson

The Origins of the Second World War (Second edition)
R. J. Overy

The Second World War in Europe
Paul MacKenzie

The French at War 1934–1944
Nicholas Atkin

Anti-Semitism before the Holocaust
Albert S. Lindemann

The Holocaust: The Third Reich and the Jews
David Engel

Germany from Defeat to Partition 1945–1963
D. G. Williamson

Britain and Europe since 1945
Alex May

Eastern Europe 1945–1969: From Stalinism to Stagnation
Ben Fowkes

Eastern Europe since 1970
Bülent Gökay

The Khrushchev Era 1953–1964
Martin McCauley

Hitler and the Rise of the Nazi Party
Frank McDonough

The Soviet Union Under Brezhnev
William Tompson

The European Union since 1945
Alasdair Blair

NINETEENTH-CENTURY BRITAIN

Britain before the Reform Acts: Politics and Society 1815–1832
Eric J. Evans

Parliamentary Reform in Britain c. 1770–1918
Eric J. Evans

Democracy and Reform 1815–1885
D. G. Wright

Poverty and Poor Law Reform in Nineteenth-Century Britain 1834–1914: From Chadwick to Booth
David Englander

The Birth of Industrial Britain: Economic Change 1750–1850
Kenneth Morgan

Chartism (Third edition)
Edward Royle

Peel and the Conservative Party 1830–1850
Paul Adelman

Gladstone, Disraeli and later Victorian Politics (Third edition)
Paul Adelman

Britain and Ireland: From Home Rule to Independence
Jeremy Smith

TWENTIETH-CENTURY BRITAIN

The Rise of the Labour Party 1880–1945 (Third edition)
Paul Adelman

The Conservative Party and British Politics 1902–1951
Stuart Ball

The Decline of the Liberal Party 1910–1931 (Second edition)
Paul Adelman

The British Women's Suffrage Campaign 1866–1928
Harold L. Smith

War & Society in Britain 1899–1948
Rex Pope

The British Economy since 1914: A Study in Decline?
Rex Pope

Unemployment in Britain between the Wars
Stephen Constantine

The Attlee Governments 1945–1951
Kevin Jefferys

The Conservative Governments 1951–1964
Andrew Boxer

Britain under Thatcher
Anthony Seldon and Daniel Collings

Britain and Empire 1880–1945
Dane Kennedy

INTERNATIONAL HISTORY

The Eastern Question 1774–1923 (Second edition)
A. L. Macfie

India 1885–1947: The Unmaking of an Empire
Ian Copland

The United States and the First World War
Jennifer D. Keene

Women and the First World War
Susan R. Grayzel

Anti-Semitism before the Holocaust
Albert S. Lindemann

The Origins of the Cold War 1941–1949 (Third edition)
Martin McCauley

Russia, America and the Cold War 1949–1991 (Second edition)
Martin McCauley

The Arab–Israeli Conflict
Kirsten E. Schulze

The United Nations since 1945: Peacekeeping and the Cold War
Norrie MacQueen

Decolonisation: The British Experience since 1945
Nicholas J. White

The Collapse of the Soviet Union
David R. Marples

WORLD HISTORY

China in Transformation 1900–1949
Colin Mackerras

Japan Faces the World 1925–1952
Mary L. Hanneman

Japan in Transformation 1952–2000
Jeff Kingston

China since 1949
Linda Benson

South Africa: The Rise and Fall of Apartheid
Nancy L. Clark and William H. Worger

Race and Empire
Jane Samson

India under Colonial Rule: 1700–1885
Douglas M. Peers

US HISTORY

American Abolitionists
Stanley Harrold

The American Civil War 1861–1865
Reid Mitchell

America in the Progressive Era 1890–1914
Lewis L. Gould

The United States and the First World War
Jennifer D. Keene

The Truman Years 1945–1953
Mark S. Byrnes

The Korean War
Steven Hugh Lee

The Origins of the Vietnam War
Fredrik Logevall

The Vietnam War
Mitchell Hall

American Expansionism 1783–1860
Mark S. Joy

The United States and Europe in the Twentieth Century
David Ryan

The Civil Rights Movement
Bruce J. Dierenfield